Forever Flowers

Flowers

A Flower Lover's Guide

to Selecting, Pressing,

and Designing

Bernice Peitzer

Published by
Krause Publications
700 East State St., Iola, WI 54990-0001
Telephone 715-445-2214
www.krause.com

Please call or write for our free catalog of publications. Our toll-free number to place
an order or obtain a free catalog is 800-258-0929 or please use our regular business
telephone 715-445-2214 for editorial comment and further information.

Library of Congress Catalog Number 99-66141
ISBN 0-87341-805-0

Drawings on pages 10-32 by Rebecca Reppert.

DEDICATION

I dedicate this book to my husband, Herb, and my two sons, Jay and Woody, for patiently watching me grow, their wives, Barbara and Wendy, and their seedlings, Aryiel, Samantha, Joel, and David.

ACKNOWLEDGMENTS

When a person succeeds in an accomplishment, it is the end result of a combination of the sharing of others. When a person is open to learning, constructive information will come.

The joy of pressing flowers and writing this book could not have been achieved without the companionship and endless encouragement from my husband, Herb, who is a master gardener. Over thirty-five years he has prepared soil, planted seeds, and helped me with his constructive suggestions in the editing of this book.

FOREWORD

This book will serve as a comprehensive information source on selecting, growing, and preserving flowers. The merging of good science with art and creativity make this horticultural text both a classic factual reference and an inspirational work.

Written from a personal perspective, Bernice shares her extensive experiences with flowers, which will captivate the reader and induce thought-provoking ideas. You will sense the miracle of plant and flower growth, gain a heightened awareness about collecting and preserving specimens here and abroad, and become confident in your own flower design potential.

Bernice's poetry, horticultural skills, and attention to detail make this botanical art form come to life.

Jonathan H. Forsell
Associate Professor
Agriculture and Natural Resources Department
Rutgers University

I am part of the Divine,
Part of the Universe of things
To which I am reborn.

I am one with the flowers and the wind,
Akin to trees and waterways,
On par with birds and beasts.

Who said that man is more?
More than more is God.

I am akin to all things
Free in flight gently touching here and
    there as I pass by.
My me is still
And the whisper of God is everywhere.

Bernice Wechsler Peitzer

TABLE OF CONTENTS

INTRODUCTION

As a child, I walked along my mother's garden path, noticing the many different flowers with their numerous shades. As I touched the colored petals, they touched my soul, and the beauty that touched me became everlasting.

I love color and design. I love nature's beauty, and learned to mix the colors of the flowers from the sky, earth, and water. I notice the natural bend of a stem and recognize the beauty in all of nature's designs.

I love touching flowers, beginning with early spring and continuing throughout the entire year. Even in winter, when all of the trees are bare, I hold a flower in my hand and admire its beauty. I fill my home with floral designs that bring the warmer months indoors.

Many years ago, in the garden section of a newspaper, there was an article on pressing flowers. I was the president of our local garden club and invited one of the members to join me in picking and pressing some of my garden varieties. We were happy with the results and started designing pictures. That year I entered an art show in the mixed media category. Most of my pictures were sold that day, and my enthusiasm for designing with pressed flowers, I knew, was to be part of my life. Soon after, I was invited to lecture at several garden clubs and women's groups.

Spiritual enlightenment—a Divine Gift.

Although I loved working with flowers, I had to learn how to cultivate the soil and which flowers I could grow that would hold their colors the best. I worked out obstacles that came along while designing new projects, and I developed new techniques so the projects in this book would be easy to make and, most of all, enjoyable.

New projects came to me through the years, and I experimented with different methods of applying techniques for them. This book will show you, step-by-step, how to develop a professional-looking project you will be proud to display in your home or give as a gift. This book also includes information on soil preparation, which flowers to plant for successful results, pressing and storing plant material, and design techniques for pressed flower arranging. Throughout the book, I share my thirty-five years of experience of designing with pressed flowers.

As you begin to work with pressed flowers, you will see a flower as you have never seen it before. You will see the many different shapes of petals, and how the blending hues harmonize into a magnificence of color. You will feel the textures of the leaves and admire their different shades of green. You will notice the combination of petals, some single, double, and trumpet-shaped. The beauty of the flowers will touch you. What a blessing. The pleasure I have found in growing, picking, and designing with flowers is as endless as one could imagine; my wish is to share this with you. Enjoy what you are doing and it will shine through.

Bernice Wechsler Peitzer

Selecting Flowers and Plants for Pressing

Spring bursts forth with a presentation of God's gifts,
Unfolding another wonderment of conception.
Releasing life.
Lifting
With hardly an interruption.
Unfolding forms
In tune with God's creative things
Surrendering
To the sequence of Divine law.
Life renewed,
And in its time of time
The deliverance is done.

Bernice Wechsler Peitzer

Suggested Flowers for Pressing

Pages 10 to 32 contain a good, basic list of flowers that can be successfully pressed and used to design an array of projects. That is not to say that there are not more you can use, so try as many different varieties as you can find; I sometimes use varieties that are not included here (as you will see in Chapter 6, Projects).

Here we discuss flowers by such characteristics as their growing habits and colors. I have included comments I feel will be helpful for you to get the best results when designing with pressed flowers. I have also suggested different projects that apply well to each flower.

When selecting flowers for pressing, remember that most require a sunny location for growing, and growing seasons vary for each region of the country. On the back of seed packages you will find a map which describes the flower to be planted, spacing of seeds, planting depth, and days of germination. These packages also indicate the best time for planting seeds. Some, like the cosmos, lobelia, and alyssum can be started indoors or in a greenhouse and then transplanted. Others, like Larkspur, must be planted directly in your garden. Some seedlings are very fragile and in their early stage should not be transplanted. This information will also be indicated on the package. (See Chapter 2 for more information on topics like seeds and growing plants and flowers.)

Why begin the book with a list of suggested flowers for pressing? If you want to grow your own flowers for pressing, this will aid you in selecting flowers to plant and grow. But, if you are planning on gathering flowers from other sources, examine this list, and then go to Chapter 3, which discusses gathering.

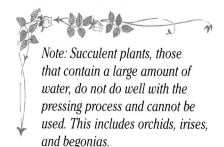

Note: Succulent plants, those that contain a large amount of water, do not do well with the pressing process and cannot be used. This includes orchids, irises, and begonias.

Alyssum (*Lobularia maritima*): Blooms in summer and autumn and is low-growing (6 to 10 inches tall) in partial sun. Rosie O'Day is rose-pink, Royal Carpet is deep violet, and Snow Cloth is white. Pressing time is between ten and fifteen days. The florets can be separated from the flowers for detail work on miniature arrangements and for small jewelry pieces.

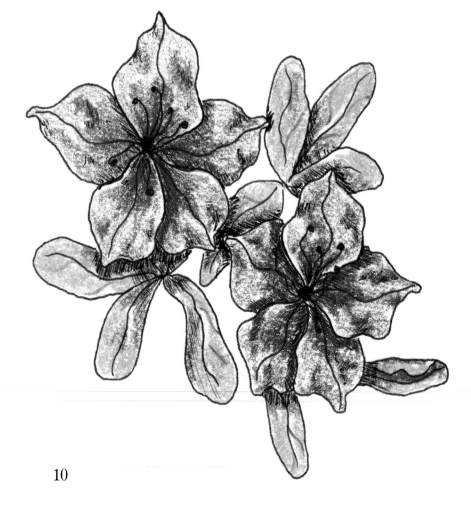

Azalea (*Ericaceae*): A bush. Blooms in spring. Grows 1 to 3 feet tall in partial sun. Colors range from red and pink to white, which can be dyed, and orange. Pressing time is between ten and fifteen days. The non-white flowers are not lasting but do look pretty on stationery.

Baby's Breath (*Gypsophila*): The paniculata variety blooms in late spring through summer. Grows 2 to 3 feet tall. Must be planted in a sunny location. It has double white flowers, touching on light pink, that can be dyed. Pressing time is between ten and fifteen days. The small stems can be separated and used to make nearly any project, including jewelry, bookmarks, and spice and perfume bottles. It has a nice airy feeling when used in pressed flower pictures.

Bachelor's Button (*Asiaticus*): Blooms in early summer. Grows about 2 feet tall. Needs sunny location. Mixed colors, but the blue is lasting (one of the few blue flowers). Pressing time is between fifteen and twenty days. Before I press it, I place it on newspaper and allow it to dry until limp. Because the resulting pressed flower is often not good, the petals can be removed and pressed separately to be used for small projects.

Bee Balm (*Oswego-tea bergamot*): Blooms in mid-summer. Grows 2 to 3 feet tall in a sunny location. Red, pink, and purple. Pressing time is between fifteen and twenty days. You can press the flowers or petals separately. The petals can be used in any project.

Bleeding Heart (*Dicentra spectabilis*): Blooms in late spring/early summer. Grows 1-1/2 feet tall in full or partial sun. Pink-red and purple-red. Makes an interesting line in an arrangement and can be used for large projects.

Bridal Wreath (*Spiraea*): A bush. Blooms late spring. Grows 4 to 5 feet tall. Needs a sunny location. Has small white clusters of flowers, which can be dyed. Pressing time is between ten and fifteen days. The florets can be separated and used for jewelry, bottles, bookmarks, and pictures.

Black-eyed Susan (*Rudbeckia hirta*): Blooms in summer. Grows 1 to 1-1/2 feet tall. Needs sunny location. Yellow-orange with a black center. The flower does fade after pressing. Pressing time is between fifteen and twenty days. Has a heavier center than most flowers, so extra weight must be used to keep it flat. It is a very showy flower that is nice to use on stationery and in pictures.

Buttercup (*Ranunculus repens*): Blooms in summer. Grows to 6 inches tall. Needs sunny location. Yellow; loses color after pressing. Pressing time is between seven and ten days. They are very dainty and are good to use on stationery or invitations.

Candytuft (*Iiberis* or *Umbellata*): Blooms late spring/early summer. Grows 9 to 15 inches tall. Needs a sunny location. Mauve, purple, bright rose, pink, and white. Pressing time is between ten and fifteen days. Could be divided for detail in smaller arrangements. Can be used for all projects.

Celosia (*Amaranthaceae*): Blooms in late spring/early summer. Grows 1 to 3-1/2 feet tall. Needs a sunny location. Red, orange, and yellow. Pressing time is between fifteen and twenty days. Good for line arrangements or spike areas in pictures.

Chrysanthemum (*Compositae*): Blooms late summer. Grows 1 to 1/1-2 feet tall. Needs a sunny location. Yellow, purple-red, and orange. Pressing time is between fifteen and twenty days. Has a dimensional appearance when using a gold or silver spray paint. It is a difficult flower to press because it retains water, yet does very well when painted (for stationery).

15

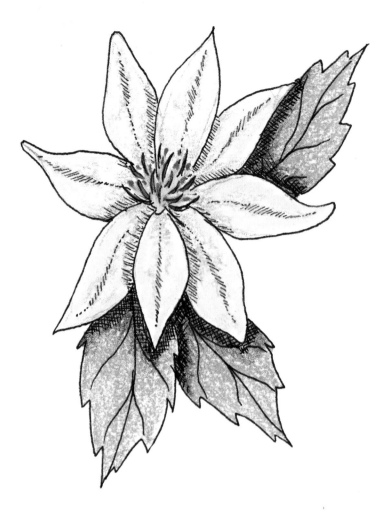

Clematis (*Clematis virginiana; c. paniculata*): A vine. Blooms late summer. Grows 6 to 10 feet tall. Needs a sunny location. White. Pressing time is between ten and fifteen days. Clusters of stems can be separated for fill-ins and can be dyed. Excellent for any project.

Columbine (*Aquilegia vulgaris*): Blooms in early summer. Grows 1-1/2 to 2 feet tall. Needs partial shade and moist soil. Crimson, pink, purple, and blue. Colors tend to fade after pressing. Pressing time is between ten and fifteen days. Fair for pictures. Mixing blue and pink flowers together on stationery or invitations is very attractive.

Coral Bells (*Heuchera sanguinea*): Blooms in late summer. Grows 1-1/2 to 2 feet tall. Needs sun or partial shade and well-drained soil. Deep or bright red bell shape. Pressing time is between ten and fifteen days. Are a nice touch to any flower arrangement and can be used for any project.

Coreopsis (*Verticillata grandfloria*): Blooms in summer. Grows 2-1/2 feet tall. Needs full sun. Bright gold; holds color well after pressing. Pressing time is between fifteen and twenty days. A showy flower to use for any project.

Cosmos (*Cosmos bipennatus*):
Blooms in mid-summer through
autumn. Grows 2 to 4 feet tall.
Needs a sunny location. Single-petal
flower. Crimson, pink, white, yellow,
and orange; retains color well.
Pressing time is between fifteen and
twenty days. Excellent for small
projects, pictures, and stationery. It
is a mainstay in my work.

Daisy (*Chrysanthemum
leucanthemum*): Blooms in
spring. Grows 1 to 1-1/2 feet
tall. Needs a sunny location.
White. Pressing time is
between ten and fifteen days.
It can be used in any project.

Delphinium (*Delphinium elatum chinensis*): Blooms in summer. Grows 3 to 4 feet tall. Needs full sun and well-drained soil. Blue, rose, pink, purple, and white. Pressing time is between fifteen and twenty days. Excellent for any project.

Dogwood (*Cornus florida*): A tree. Blooms in spring. Needs partial shade. White and pink flowers; some may turn ivory after pressing. Pressing time is between fifteen and twenty days. Good for pictures and stationery.

Ferns: Many varieties. Available in spring to late summer. Usually grow in partially to fully shaded areas. Many different sizes and shapes. Shades of green will differ with each variety. Pressing time is between ten and fifteen days. Provide an excellent background for all projects.

Forget-me-not (*Myosotis alpestis c blue ball*): Blooms in mid-spring/early summer. Grows 6 to 9 inches tall in partial sun. Blue, pale pink, and white. Pressing time is between ten and fifteen days. Good for any project.

Fruit blossoms: Including cherry (shown here), apple, and peach. Bloom in early spring. Need sunny location. Abundance of white and light pink flowers. Could be pressed individually or in small clusters. Pressing time is between ten and fifteen days. Excellent flowers to dye and use with any project.

Gloriosa Daisy (*Rudbeckia hirta-Lili-aacse-Glory Lily*): Blooms in summer. Grows 1 to 1-1/2 feet tall. Needs moist soil. Yellow, orange, and red. Colors fade after pressing. Pressing time is between fifteen and twenty days; has thick center and needs extra weight during pressing. Flowers can be dyed. Fair for pictures.

Goldenrod (*Solidago canadensis*): Blooms in late summer. Grows 3 to 4 feet tall. Needs a sunny location. Yellow spike flowers, which lose their color after pressing but can be used for spikes in an arrangement. Pressing time is between fifteen and twenty days. Heavy in feeling and can be pressed in small pieces. Good to use for height.

Grasses: Spring and fall. Important background or fill-in for pressed flower projects; have nice light, airy feeling. Can be found anywhere. Pressing time is between ten and fifteen days. Excellent in any arrangement and project.

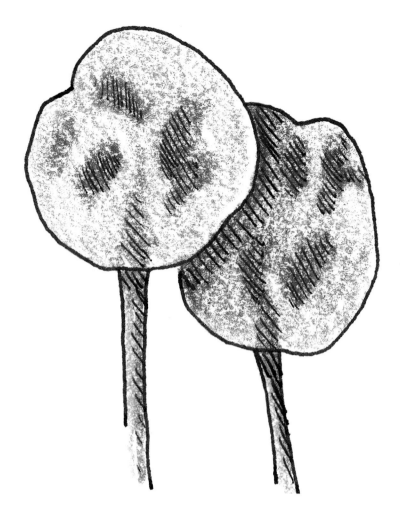

Honesty (*Lunaria biennis*): The "money plant." Flower blooms in spring, "silver dollar" in fall. Grows 1-1/2 feet tall. Needs well-drained soil and partial shade. Little black seeds within pod can be replanted in fall. Violet-lilac to purple bloom. If you cut the flower you will not get the silver heart-shaped heads; the silvery seed heads are also good for pressing (or for dried arrangements). Pressing time is between fifteen and twenty days. Makes a dramatic statement in a picture with a black velvet or dark background.

Honeysuckle (*Lonicera x americana*): A vine. Blooms in summer in partial sun. Tube-like clusters are creamy white. Foliage is deep green. Pressing time for flowers alone is between ten to fifteen days. Pressing time for vine is between fifteen and twenty days. Twist the young growth before it is pressed; the curved shape creates an artistic line for pictures or stationery. Young growth does best, because older branches become too woody. Flowers also can be used in potpourri (see page 49).

Hydrangea (*Hydrangeaceae*): Blooms in summer. Shrubs grow to 6 feet tall. Needs a sunny location. Blue and purple. Pressing time is between ten and fifteen days. Good for potpourri (see page 49) or any project.

Larkspur (*Ranunculaceae*): Blooms in summer. Grows 1-1/2 to 3 feet tall. Needs well-drained, sandy soil. Blue, pink, rose, and white. Pressing time is between ten and twelve days. Good flower to use in any arrangement because it is showy.

Leaves: Many types of leaves can be used, including oak, red maple, beech, honey locust, chestnut, weeping willow, and elm. In the spring, the leaves are small, growing into larger sizes mid-summer. In the fall they begin to change color into red-yellow combinations. They can be picked at any time before frost. Pressing time is between ten and fifteen days. Can be used in pictures, on stationery, and in photo albums.

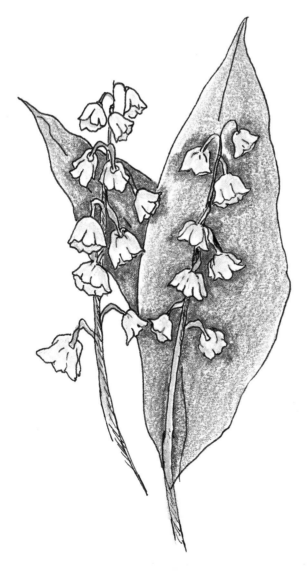

Lily-of-the-valley (*Consolida ambigua*): Blooms in early spring. Grows 6 to 12 inches tall. Needs partial sun. White bell-shaped flowers, which may turn ivory. Pressing time is between fifteen and twenty days. Excellent for any project, especially wedding invitations.

Lobelia (*L. erinus Campanulaceae*): Blooms in summer. Grows up to 6 inches tall in partially sunny location. Blue, white, and pink. Pressing time is between ten and fifteen days. Can be pressed in little clusters with the leaves or individually. Presses and keeps color well. Excellent for any project. There are not many blue flowers with lasting color, so it is excellent to use when you need blue as an accent in an arrangement.

Lythrum (*Lythraceae*): Blooms in summer. Grows 4 to 5 feet tall. Needs moist, heavy soil and partial shade. Red-purple spikes; will eventually turn to light pink after pressing. Flowers can be separated. Pressing time is between fifteen and twenty days. Excellent for pictures, stationery, or any miniature arrangement.

Narcissus/Paper Whites (*Amaryllidaceae*): Blooms in spring. Grows 1 to 1-1/2 feet tall. Needs moist soil. White. There are some miniature varieties (*asturiensis*). Pressing time is between fifteen and twenty days. Excellent for pictures, stationery, and potpourri (see page 49). Dramatic on a dark background.

Pansy (*Viola tricolor*): Blooms in late spring/early summer. Grows 4 to 6 inches tall. There are smaller varieties (viola and Johnny-jump-ups). Needs well-drained soil. Blooms in all colors, but they do not last after pressing. Pressing time is between ten and fifteen days. Can be used on stationery or invitations.

Phlox (*Poemonia ceae*): Blooms in mid-spring/early summer. Grows 6 to 12 inches tall. Needs well-drained area. Purple and white; does not keep color well. Nice in clusters. Pressing time is between ten and fifteen days. Use on stationery and invitations. Can be dyed.

Poppy (*Papaver*): Blooms in summer. 4 to 8 inches tall, but some varieties grow 1-1/2 to 2 feet tall. Needs full sun in well-drained soil. Very fragile. Scarlet, pink, red, purple, peach, salmon, and yellow; does not hold color well after pressing. When pressed, has a translucent, silky appearance. Pressing time is between ten and fifteen days. Attractive on a dark background.

Queen Anne's Lace (*Daucus carota*): Known as the "wild carrot." Blooms in summer. Grows 3 to 4 feet tall. Needs sunny location. White. Pressing time is between ten and fifteen days. Excellent for any project. Flower that has already bloomed and is folded can be used in a picture. Excellent for detail when florets are separated. Can be dyed.

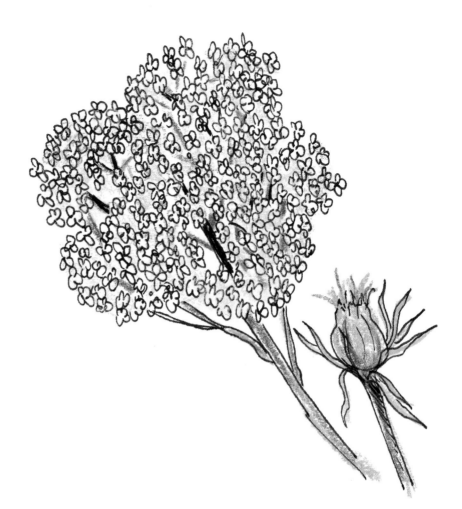

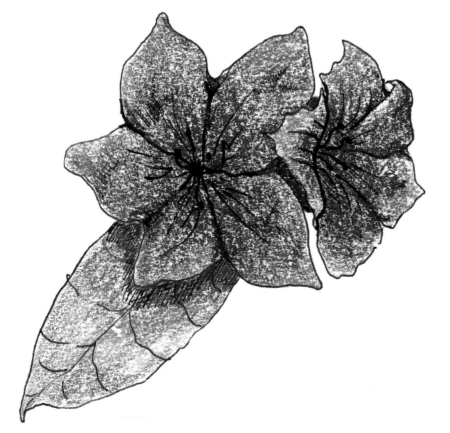

Rhododendron (*Rhododendron*): A shrub. Blooms in spring. Can grow to 10 feet tall. Diameter of the flower can be up to 3 inches. Needs shade, acidic soil, and lots of mulch. Many varieties. Purple, red, and orange. Showy flower. Purple variety is beautiful, but loses its color after pressing. Pressing time is fifteen to twenty days. Other varieties can be dyed and are excellent for pictures or stationery.

Rose (*Rosa*): A bush. Blooms in summer. Needs full sun and well-drained soil. Wide range of varieties, including miniature, and colors. Pressing time is between fifteen and twenty days. Fair in holding color after pressing. Single-petal Betsy Prior Rose is best to use for pictures and stationery. Nice for pictures, stationery, and potpourri (see page 49). The petals could be separated and then reassembled (see page 47).

Sea Pink (*Dianthus*): Blooms in spring. Grows 8 inches tall. Needs full sun. Rose ball-shaped flower; turns purple when pressed. Fair in keeping color. Good for stationery.

Snapdragon (*Antirrhinum majus*): Blooms in late summer/autumn. Depending on variety, will grow 3 inches to 2 feet tall. Needs sunny location. Crimson, lavender, pink, orange, yellow, and white. Press individually. Pressing time is between ten and fifteen days. Good for pictures and stationery.

Verbena (*VervBena Species*): Blooms in mid-summer/mid-autumn. Grows 1 to 1-1/2 feet tall. Needs sunny location and well-drained soil. Rose, pink, blue, purple, and white. Holds color moderately well. Flowers bloom in clusters. I press the flowers separately. Pressing time is between ten and fifteen days. Size shrinks after pressing. Excellent for all projects, especially jewelry, bottles, and bookmarks.

31

Vines: Spring/fall. Found in woods, on fences, and in fields. Young tendrils wind around their supports. Pressing time is between ten and fifteen days. Vines are good to use for all types of arrangements, and young spring tendrils create an excellent touch for any project.

Zinnia (*Zinna elegans*): Blooms in late summer/autumn. Grows 1 to 3 feet tall. Needs sunny location in well-drained soil. Many colors. After picking, let flower wilt slightly with the head on newspaper, then press. Pressing time between fifteen and twenty days. Can be dyed as cluster; head is pretty. Attractive when sprayed with gold or silver for stationery.

SELECTING AND PLANTING SEEDS

Seeds planted in my heart
Begin their journey toward the light.
Flowers birthing to full bloom
Ready to be shared.
                    Bernice Wechsler Peitzer

There is much preparation and planning to be done if you are going to grow your own flowers for pressing. From selecting seeds, to transplanting seedlings and preparing your garden, you will experience the joy of "doing it yourself."

Flower Seeds

Seeds come in different shapes and sizes, from tiny alyssum seeds that blow away if you breathe on them to larger zinnia seeds that are easy to handle. Most flower seeds have seed coats that soften quickly on contact with moisture. The coat protects the inner seed from damage. Germination is the process of seeds sprouting roots and leaves and is one of the great miracles of nature. For most seeds, three conditions must be met before germination occurs: adequate moisture, suitable temperature, and air (oxygen). First, moisture is necessary to soften the seed coat and allow the embryo, the undeveloped plant, to expand and grow. If the soil is waterlogged for an extended period, though, the seeds will die. For this reason, it is best to start seeds in a potting mix that drains well to allow air to enter the soil. Second, a suitable temperature is needed to break dormancy so the seed can sprout. Finally, air is required for the seeds to live.

Seeds come in many shapes and sizes. Shown at left are morning glory seeds, and marigold seeds are shown at right.

Pellets, Tapes, and Seed Packets

Almost every year there seems to be a new way to plant seeds. Seed pellets, seed tapes, and other methods are said to make seed starting easier and more reliable.

Seed pellets are probably the least gimmicky of these alternative seed-sowing systems. The pellet is a clay coating around small seeds that make them larger and easier to handle. The coating dissolves on contact with moisture and the seed germinates unhindered. Pelleted seeds tend to look like they have been manufactured, which might bother the gardening purist, yet they do make it easier to sow small-seed flowers.

Tip:

Do not use the entire seed packet in one sowing. Save some seeds to fill in bare spots after plants come up. This will also stager the blooming time; the flowers will bloom at different intervals in the growing season.

33

Seed tapes are seed-bound into a transparent, biodegradable material, prespaced at regular distances. The material dissolves quickly after it comes in contact with moisture. Seed tapes save time because you don't have to thin seedlings out later, but they have some disadvantages: they are more expensive than conventional seeds from packets and might not get a high rate of germination, resulting in wide gaps between plants. Tapes can also be a nuisance to plant because they are usually packed folded with sharp corners, so they buckle out of the soil when you stretch the tape in the furrow.

Seed packets have been significantly improved with the introduction of foil packaging. These packets are moisture-proof and keep seeds fresher longer. Some seeds deteriorate quickly, and the traditional paper packets may allow seeds to lose viability. Under controlled conditions, seeds in moisture-proof packets maintain germination until the seal is broken. You get better value with a seed packet because it contains more seeds at less cost compared to seed tapes and other systems.

Seeds: Seed Rack or Mail Order?

The advantage of rack displays in most local stores is convenience. It is easy to go down to the nearest garden supply store which offers the best brands and best selection of traditional, established varieties. It is wise to purchase early in the season, because there is a greater selection than late in the season (seed companies do not refill the displays because they have to take back the unsold seeds). The major disadvantage is that you cannot get special and heirloom varieties, because these are not available to the mass-market.

Seed catalogs number in the hundreds. Some are filled with color pictures, while others are specialized and appeal to certain interested gardeners. Along with variety listings, descriptions, and pictures, you will find valuable hints. Some catalogs are specialist and carry seeds that are not found in the average garden supply store.

Seed rack or mail-order catalog? There are advantages and disadvantages to both!

Saving Seeds from Your Garden

Many gardeners like to save seeds from their garden plants to use the next season. Based on my experience, it is best to start with fresh seeds; it is better not to save seeds unless you have a variety that is unobtainable from normal sources, but it can be done (see below). Plants grown from seeds from your own garden may give unpredictable results. Seeds saved from hybrids, an offspring of one plant crossed with another, produce inferior results the second season. In general, it is best not to save seeds from hybrids because they don't produce a high-quality flower.

When you have more experience, though, you can try to gather seeds yourself and store them until the next growing season. It is best to wait until the flowers on the growing plant turn completely brown and crumble when touched; the seeds must have time to mature. When I remove the flower heads,

I keep a cardboard box under the flower. Because the flower is completely dry, the seeds will fall right into the box. The seeds can be stored in a cool area in a paper bag or box (not plastic). Make sure the storing area is not damp.

Storing and Testing Leftover Seeds

Most seed companies are generous with the quantities of seeds they provide in packets. You may find that after planting you have a lot of leftover seeds in opened packets.

To store seeds, place packets in a wide-mouth jar that can be sealed with a tight-fitting lid. Put two heaping tablespoons of powdered milk in a paper envelope and place it in the jar. The powdered milk will absorb moisture from the air inside the jar, keeping the seeds dry. Seal the jar and store in the vegetable bin of your refrigerator (to maintain viability, seeds must be kept cool and dry). High temperatures and humidity deteriorate seeds quickly and reduce the rate of germination. Seeds can be kept in such a manner for up to two years.

To see if the seeds are viable (they can produce the quality of plants you want), select about ten seeds and place them on a moist paper towel. Put the towel inside a sealed plastic bag in a warm location (the plastic bag prevents the paper towel from drying out too quickly). After ten days, count the number of seeds that have germinated. In general, one to three out of ten is considered poor, four to six good, and seven to ten is excellent.

Starting Seeds Indoors

Some seeds can be planted directly in your garden (see page 38), but others should be started indoors. Starting seeds indoors will give you a good start, especially when your growing season is short.

Plants can be started from seeds in many different ways, but any type of container about 2 to 3 inches tall is suitable. Jiffy pots, which are small sections you fill with a starter mixture—one-third peat moss and two-thirds perlite or vermiculite—work well. This mixture can be purchased prepared from your local nursery. Some gardeners use cardboard egg boxes to start difficult-to-grow seeds like larkspur; these plants do not like to be handled too much, and this way the cardboard sections can be spaced correctly. The cardboard sections can be planted separately, so they do not damage the seedlings.

If the container is made from fiber or peat moss, it must be watered before working with your seed mixture. Make sure there is good drainage in whatever container you choose and don't forget to cover starter trays with plastic (you should put jiffy pots or cardboard boxes in a tray, or flat. Line the tray with stones or gravel.

One of the biggest problems with growing seeds indoors is maintaining moisture; seeds grown in small peat pots and soil blocks tend to lose moisture rapidly. If a seedling is deprived of moisture for only a few hours, it will probably wilt and die. Follow directions carefully on the peat moss package.

When watering seeds in trays, apply water in a fine mist or add water to the tray, but do not pour water directly on seeds because it will disturb the soil surface and hinder germination. To prevent rapid moisture loss, enclose trays or pots of newly planted seeds in a clear plastic bag; it will help prevent evaporation and keep the soil moist.

Once seedlings begin to appear, remove the plastic covering. You can take trays outside, but place them in a partially shaded area at first until they are ready to be planted in the ground. Gradually put them in stronger light over the next few weeks. If the nights are cold, it is best to bring them in. Most plants will grow at normal room temperature (60 to 75 degrees F).

Once the first set of leaves appears, you can fertilize it with a weak solution once a week. Be careful not to over fertilize, because it will kill your seedlings.

Label the tray with the names of the plants in it, using such materials as plastic sticks or old venetian blinds that can be used later in your outdoor garden area where they will be planted, or you can also attach masking tape to the tray.

Proper Light

A major reason for poor quality of home-grown transplants is inadequate light. Transplants become spindly and stretch when they do not receive enough light. Seedlings should be exposed to about six hours of sunlight each day except those that prefer heavy shade, which will be indicated on the seed packet. When growing transplants on windowsills, raise the pots to the level of the window pane. Also consider placing an aluminum foil reflector on the dark side of the seedlings so that light is bounced back to increase illumination. A simple reflector can be made by wrapping kitchen foil around a piece of cardboard.

Plant lights that simulate sunshine can be used to supplement natural light. Timers are available that automatically turn the lights on and off. Set seedlings a few inches away from light to produce good growth and give them at least twelve hours of artificial light each day.

Light units are available in a wide range of styles, sizes, and prices. Standard fluorescent fixtures can be fitted with special plant "grow lights." Table-top models provide enough light for a tray of seedlings. Free-standing floor units accommodate up to eight trays.

Preventing Disease

The biggest killer of seedlings is damping-off disease, which is caused by a fungus present in unsterilized soil, dirty pots, and unclean seeds. Over-watering, poor ventilation, poor light, and high temperatures help encourage the harmful fungus. It can attack seeds sown indoors or outdoors, but is most destructive to indoor sowings, often killing seedlings before they have a chance to emerge from the soil. Treating seeds with a fungicide such as

Captan before you plant can help avoid infestations and prevent disease. Using new or clean seed-starting pots or trays and sterile potting soil will also help prevent damping-off.

Transplanting

(Note: Before transplanting your seedlings, see below for information on preparing your garden.)

Wait until there is a second set of leaves on your seedlings before you transplant and thin them out. Use a spoon or fork to transplant the seedlings. It is best to handle them by the leaves, not the root system, and it is important to be gentle and not damage them. When transplanting, the seedlings must be watered thoroughly. Mist them with a soluble fertilizer. Before you plant them in your garden, be absolutely sure that you will not have any more frost. If you are not sure, it is best to leave them in the trays for another four weeks (to allow the flowers to absorb the fertilizer through the leaves and root system).

Garden Preparation

It is important to turn the soil over in your garden each spring with a roto-tiller, pitchfork, or spade before planting and transplanting. Spread a 1-inch layer of peat moss, compost, or leaf mulch over the bed and mix in a dry fertilizer. The soil should be tested to make sure the pH level is 6.5 (see below). (See the following page for more information on preparing the garden bed.)

How to Take a Soil Sample

Taking a soil sample is an important step in ensuring a successful garden. Some soil is too dry, damp, or sandy for certain types of flowers and plants; you must fit the needs of your planting in order to get results you will be proud of. Analyzing your soil's fertility lets you apply supplementary nutrients to suit the needs of the plants you wish to grow. Proper lime and fertilizer application reduces wasted nutrients and stress on the plants.

A pH test indicates the level of soil acidity (pH less than 7.0). Turf, flowers, and most vegetables grow best in soils that are slightly acidic (pH 6.0 to 6.5). If the pH of the soil is too low, add lime before starting a new lawn or garden to give it time to react with the soil to raise the pH. Raising the soil pH too high (above 7.0) can decrease the availability of some nutrients; therefore, adding more lime is not beneficial. Basically, plants and flowers will only thrive when the pH level is correct for them. To find what pH is right for the plants and flowers you intend to grow, check the seed packet, the label on the plants (if they were purchased at a nursery), or with your county's agricultural agent.

You have a choice for testing your soil. A pH test is done by a lab or with a special kit sold at a garden shop. It can also be sent to an agricultural agent or an agricultural cooperative lab.

Tip:

You can apply slow-release fertilizers when planting seeds, but do not use fast-acting fertilizers; they may burn tender seedlings. After applying fertilizer, wait seven to ten days before planting.

Tip:

Never walk on garden soil where seedlings are or will be planted, because heavy footprints compact soil and can ruin a well-prepared seed bed. Instead, use paths between rows or walk on planks.

To measure soil fertility accurately, you must prepare a representative sample; meaning you must sample more than one spot within the area of concern. For large plantings or areas that are different, such as lawns, and vegetable gardens, separate samples will allow proper recommendations for each site because different areas within your garden may require varied soil mixtures (for instance if you want to grow something specific in a particular area that requires an acid or alkaline soil). Before starting, determine that the soil is dry enough to sample by squeezing a handful. It is dry enough if it crumbles when you open your fist.

Directions for taking a soil sample will be included with the kit, or the agency you use can give you instructions, but, in general, you will begin sampling by making a vertical cut to a depth of 6 to 8 inches with a spade or trowel. Make a second cut at a 45-degree angle to the first, removing the wedge-shaped section and setting it aside. Make another vertical cut as deep as the first, 1/2 inch from it to get a fresh, uncontaminated sample.

Place a piece of this slice in a clean bucket and replace the remaining portion of the slice back in the ground. Repeat this procedure five to eight times within the area to be tested (the larger the area, the more slices you should take). Thoroughly mix the soil in the bucket, removing any plant material and large stones.

For a pH test, place 1/2 cup of the mix in a clean container. For the complete test, keep a pint of the soil mix. The complete test involves taking samples from different places in your sowing area and mixing them together for a composite reading for your garden; the soil composition may vary throughout your garden.

After this is done, call your local Cooperative Extension Office (consult your telephone directory) to find out whether pH testing is available before you obtain the sample. Bring or mail 1/2 cup of soil to the office.

A test for major nutrients can be performed for a fee from many universities or state land grants. This test includes recommendations for correcting pH and magnesium, phosphorous, and potassium levels. It is recommended to have this soil test done every five years.

Planting Seeds Outdoors

Gardeners sometimes kill by kindness. One common mistake is overdoing the preparation of a seed bed. Don't rake the soil until it is fine as dust; that is the way to make mud pies. When the soil dries out after watering, the seeds will be imprisoned in a tight crust of soil. Also, don't tenderly cover seeds with loose soil. Seeds must have contact with soil in order to grow properly; there should be no air pockets. If your soil has heavy clay, and you don't want to improve the soil in the entire garden, add compost or other organic material to the row to be planted. Finally, don't rush the season. The warmer the soil, the better the chances for success.

The old rule of thumb is to plant seeds at a depth equal to four times

Tip:

Firm the soil over planted seeds with your foot or the back of the spade, but don't compress the soil too much; press just enough to eliminate air pockets. This process will ensure that the seeds are making contact with the soil.

their diameter, but check the planting information on the back of each seed packet for correct depths. In wet weather or in heavy soils, plant shallow, but if soils are light and sandy and dry weather is anticipated, plant deeper.

There are ways to prevent drying out and crusting of the soil surface. Some gardeners cover soil rows with burlap sacks and sprinkle with water as necessary, but with sacks there is always the danger of forgetting to water the seeds for a few days. If the seedlings do not get sufficient water on a regular basis, they will wither and die.

A one-eighth mulch of vermiculite, bark, or sawdust will prevent crusting and reduce the frequency of sprinkling. In windy weather, it is a good idea to contain the mulch with a cover to prevent the soil from blowing away.

Clear plastic is a good mulch, but close watch for the emergence of seedlings is needed. Plastic must be removed as soon as seedlings show. Make a shallow trough and plant seeds at the bottom. Cover the trough with clear plastic only, at an angle so water can run off.

Sowing

Sowing is planting seeds at their proper distance and depth as described on the seed packet. First, wet the soil. Then, use a pencil to make your seed lines for planting by marking the area where you will plant seeds. Leave approximately 1 inch between the seeds (or seedlings) because they need a good amount of air and light. Some seeds are very tiny, so if a few slip into your seed planting mixture while sowing, leave them because you will be thinning them out later for proper spacing (because they need the correct amount of sunlight and air).

Growing Times and Blooming

Refer to your seed packets for growing and blooming times for your flowers. Refer to Chapter 1 for a listing of common varieties used in pressed flower projects. For the best results, contact your local agricultural agent.

You are well on your way to having a beautiful garden, not only to enjoy, but to use the flowers you grow!

Certain seeds, including snapdragon, annual poppy, alyssum, candytuft, California poppy, and baby's breath, can be planted in your garden in September. Make sure you follow the instructions for planting that is applicable to your local area. After frost, cover them with mulch.

3

Gathering Flowers and Plant Material

Gathering rainbows
Colors pressed between the
pages
Remembrance
Of soul touching soul.
Everlasting flowers
Everlasting love
Eternity.

Bernice Wechsler Peitzer

The Basics

Tip:

Although it is fun to find areas to pick flowers, you must be careful not to pick them on private property, in parks, or other property you do not own.

Tip:

If you live in an area where there are white-tailed deer, you must cover yourself properly against ticks. Also, be aware of poison ivy, as well as yellow, white, or red poison sumac berries .

The best time to pick flowers for pressing is in the mid-afternoon, when the sun is bright and the morning dew has evaporated. The flower heads are open and are at their driest point of the day. This means you will get the freshest and most vivid color to use in your designs.

Because mid-afternoon may not be convenient for gathering, there might be some flowers you will pick at other times. When it is necessary to cut the flowers early in the day, place four or five layers of newspaper on a flat surface and spread the cut flowers with the stems so they face downward on the paper. In most cases, the flowers can be left to dry thoroughly for a few hours. Use this method when it has rained the night before and you want to cut certain varieties that are still wet. It is important to watch your picked flowers; the petals should not begin to curl or shrivel before you remove them from the newspaper for pressing.

When picking flowers on a very hot, humid afternoon, I pick and press small quantities at a time. It is shocking to see how quickly they wither on a hot, humid day! If there is an interruption, put the picked flowers in a shaded area or under a picnic table, but do not leave them for very long because the heat of the day will wither the flowers quickly and they cannot be used.

Choosing Shears

When cutting flowers, you will need strong, comfortable, sharp shears. When I cut flowers, I like to use a particular kind of flower shear in which the cutting blades firmly hold the flowers. They come in handy, eliminating possible scratches on your hands from thorny bushes or thicket areas. Here are some shears I have had success with:

✻ #426A12 are Joyce Chen Unlimited Scissors. They have flexible handles, which are comfortable right- or left-handed. The all-purpose blade cuts everything from flower stems to florist's wire, paper, and ribbons. They cut just about anything you need while working with pressed flowers.

✻ #427A12 are from Joshua Roth Limited. These also have flexible handles. They have long, slender, carbon-steel blades that are great for getting between foliage to cut exactly what you want. The blades are extremely sharp, giving a very clean cut.

✻ #460A10, from Dorothy Biddle Service, are cut-and-hold shears. They are made by Victorinox (the same company that makes Swiss Army Knives). These have stainless-steel blades to cleanly cut flower stems. They will hold the stem after it has been cut, which saves having to grasp the cut pieces with your other hand in hard-to-get-at areas. They are ideal for cutting flowers and foliage.

Shears for cutting flowers. From the top: Shears from Joyce Chen Unlimited, Joshua Roth Limited, and Dorothy Biddle Service.

Cutting Flowers

Cut the area of the flower you will need for your particular project (see Chapter 6 for ideas). You can cut only the flower head (without the stem) or the stem. Hold the stem firmly with your non-cutting hand, below the section you are going to cut. Some shears, like those from Dorothy Biddle described above, will hold the stem after it has been cut, which is a great help in tight areas.

Important Tips

Before cutting, it is important to gently press the center of the flower head, holding it between your thumb and index finger, to feel if there are any wet or damp areas that have not dried. If any wet or damp areas remain, the flower will rot during the conditioning time (the time it takes the flowers to be pressed); flowers must be completely dry before pressing. If the flowers or leaves are not thoroughly dry, they can cause black spots to appear and should not be used in any of your projects. The time element for the flowers to be completely dry depends on the time of day the flowers are picked, the size of the flower, and the amount of petals each flowers has (see Chapter 1). If it rained the night before you cut them, flowers will absorb more water than with the morning dew, so place them on newspaper (as described on the next page). Make sure they do not touch each other (this prolongs drying time).

*Warning: Be aware of insects that may have a home in the basket you use to pick flowers. Also, **research the area**, making sure there are no poisonous trees or plants before you pick the flowers.*

When preparing to gather flowers, make sure you have good shears, a basket for gathering the material, and you are wearing gardening gloves.

Tip:

Mid-afternoon is the best time to gather your flowers, and bees agree with you (that is also the best time for pollination). Bees also burrow in the ground, so be very cautious when you are weeding or picking flowers. Let them have the right-of-way!

Tip:

During the growing season, pick as many varieties of flowers as you can. Do not be afraid to try new flowers or interesting shapes of flowers you have not pressed before. Your designs will take on a different look with each flower, leaf, or grass you use.

Test flowers with your fingers every half hour to see if they are dry. The newspaper will absorb some of the water, but if the newspaper gets too wet, change it every half hour.

You will be surprised and delighted where you will find wildflowers growing! When I travel I always pack a few plastic bags with ties and my shears. Flowers in a bag should last one to two hours, but when there will be a longer time span, I usually dampen paper toweling or newspaper, not enough that it is dripping, and place it inside the plastic bag. This keeps the moisture in for a short duration. If the flowers begin to wilt, put only the stems, and not the flower heads, in a bucket of water when you return home. This will refresh them prior to pressing and will prevent the flower petals from curling. Watch them carefully; when the flower heads begin to lift, that indicates they are ready to be pressed. This method also applies to any foliage you have collected that you cannot immediately press. **When taking them out of the water, be sure that the stems and flowers are not wet.** Of course, it is always better to press the flowers as soon as they are picked if they are dry.

After you have picked your flowers, keep a record of the date, location, and variety of the flowers. This will be helpful for the following years to remind you of a favorite flower or greenery you found and where you might find them again.

Chapter 4

PRESSING AND STORING FLOWERS AND PLANT MATERIAL

Picture Enchantment

Like a goddess the sun comes up from behind the mountain
Her mighty head high and her long thin arms outstretched
lighting the day with her beauty beaming with love and life
Using the dew in the morning as a jewel, the fragrance of pine
     as perfume, and the rainbow of wealth as a crown
She walks gently over the sky.
Her radiance traveling from each leaf on the tallest tree then
     sloping gently through the branches and leaves with a ray
     of conscious beauty.
She touches the flowers with her dainty shades of color, and
     glides through rustic fences and golden hay.
Quietly she finds a resting place and gently begins to fade,
     pulling in her expanded glow.
She bows her head gracefully.
Silently twilight descends.

                                        Bernice Wechsler Peitzer

Now that you have gathered plants and flowers, it is time to press them! Before discussing *how* to press them, you first need to be introduced to the different devices that can be used for pressing. When choosing the pressing method, consider the weight and size of each flower. Also, consider what type of flower arrangement you are going to design (see Chapter 5 for design ideas and Chapter 6 for projects).

Flower Presses

It is easy and convenient for a beginner to use a flower press. I recommend taking a flower press along when you are going on a nature walk through the woods, fields, or meadows. Leave an extra press in your car for surprising finds.

Sunstone, Inc. in Cooperstown, New York, manufactures different varieties of presses (see Resources). The company makes a traditional flower press out of plywood with screws and wing nuts that can be tightened a little bit each day, which prevents air from entering during the drying process. These are especially good for pressing large and bulky flowers. There is also a Velcro strap press that is designed for use by children who might find the hardware too difficult to manipulate. This type is easy to carry on hikes and take along when traveling because there isn't hardware protruding that could damage a suitcase or knapsack.

Flower presses from Sunstone, Inc., clockwise, from the top: The Gardener's Press, The Leaf & Flower Press, and The Nature Press.

Homemade Flower Press

Here is a simple flower press you can make yourself.

You will need

Two 12- x 15-inch pieces of
  plywood
Sandpaper
Newspaper
Two 12-inch long bungee
  cords

1. Use the sandpaper to smooth the edges of the two plywood pieces.
2. Fold large sheets of newspaper to measure 11 x 13 inches.
3. Center the newspaper on one piece of plywood. Add more pieces of folded newspaper until the "stack" measures approximately two inches. (You need at least two inches above and below each layer of flowers.) Place a layer of flowers on the newspapers.
4. Repeat Step 3 until all of your flowers are layered on the newspaper.
5. Put the second piece of plywood over the last layer of newspaper.
6. Secure the layers with the bungee cords.
7. Place the press in a cool, dry place.
8. Check the flowers after five days. If the newspaper has absorbed a lot of moisture, replace it with dry sheets. Replace the flowers and secure again with the bungee cords.

Telephone Books and Newspapers

Another pressing method can be done with telephone books—the larger the better—which are very absorbent. (Do not use magazines, because they usually have a shiny surface and are not as absorbent.) When my business started to grow very quickly, I needed a large supply of telephone books, so I contacted the telephone company and was told that it had a supply of obsolete telephone books. Try that, or ask your friends and family for old books.

With this method, I use fresh newspapers between the pages. Begin by folding a large sheet in half and then in half again, so that the end result is approximately 7-1/2 x 10-1/2 inches. This size will fit between most telephone book pages very well. It is best not to use colored newspaper, because some of the color might get on the petals. I do not like to use paper toweling, because its embossed imprint will remain on the petals when pressed. Also, any color on them will possibly be transferred to the petals.

General Notes

It is very important for leaves, stems, or flowers not to extend beyond the newspaper and out of the telephone book or flower press. Naturally, if they are not placed between the newspaper they will be crushed. When placing the flowers, they must not touch one another; they must have their own space. If the flowers touch one another, the petals will stick together.

It is not wise to press many pages of flowers in one book or press. As a rule of thumb, place no more than three pages of flowers in a large telephone book because this will ensure the flowers will remain flat. If too many flowers are pressed in the same book, the paper will absorb too much water, causing the flowers to rot.

Make a quick and easy flower press with telephone books and newspapers.

Make sure the stems do not run off of the paper.

Pressing Flowers With a Flower Press

First, place a piece of cardboard on the bottom piece of plywood. Put two pieces of blotting paper on top of that. Now, place the flowers on the blotting paper.

After you have placed a few flowers on the blotting paper, cover them with two additional pieces of paper.

Cover the blotting paper with a piece of cardboard. Repeat this process until you have placed all of your flowers. The last layer should be a piece of cardboard.

(Shown here is the Gardener's Press from Sunstone, Inc.)

Cover the final piece of cardboard with the top piece of plywood.

After the top piece of plywood is in place, secure and tighten the Velcro straps.

Before You Begin

A very important point is to make sure that the area in which you place the books or flower press is cool and dry. An area that is very humid will cause the flowers to rot. A damp basement is not the place to keep the books for pressing, or for filing away your already pressed flowers.

It is also important to place weights like cinder blocks or empty telephone books on the books. This will ensure that the flowers will remain flat; if the books do not remain flat, the flowers inside will fall apart when you remove them.

Press many different varieties and more flowers than you think you will use. It is always better to have more than to find later that you need certain varieties that are long out of season.

Whether you are using a flower press or telephone book, in the long run, it is easier to press the same varieties together. They have to be stored, and

Tip:

Consult Chapter 1 for approximate pressing times.

by pressing them together, it will save you time. You might want to label each book. One way of doing this is to have labels or slips extending from the telephone book, with the name of each flower variety you are pressing. In this way, you can keep track of the varieties you are working on, and if you need a certain variety quickly you know where to find it.

There are times when you may need a bud or smaller flower, or you may want to use a flower that retains a lot of water. This method removes a lot of moisture before it can be pressed so it does not rot. A little trick that works well is to allow the flower to get nearly dry. Place the flower face down on newspaper so it becomes limp. You have to watch very carefully so you do not allow the petals to dry out completely and become so brittle that they cannot be used at all. Now they are ready to be pressed in the usual manner.

Methods for Pressing Flowers

There are three different methods of pressing flowers. The first method is pressing the flowers with the stem attached. The second method is pressing them without the stem. The third method is pressing the petals separately. The method you use depends on the design you choose (see Chapter 5 for different line arrangements). Note: You can use any pressing device with any method.

Method 1

The first method, which I use for the bulk of my work, is to press flowers with the stem intact. The stems do not have to be perfectly straight; when the stem is curved, it will lend itself to a free flow as you design your arrangement.

Keep the stem's thickness in mind while pressing. A stem that is thin, for example a cosmos, larkspur, or lily-of-the-valley, can easily be pressed together with the flower head. Because a flower is dainty when it is pressed, a stem that is too heavy in feeling will create an imbalance, making the composition of your design look unnatural. In addition, if you are creating a picture and the stem is too thick, the glass will break when framing it and the petals will reach toward the glass like metal shavings drawn to a magnet; the petals of the flower will eventually break, destroying your arrangement. If the flower has a thick stem, remove it from the flower and press it in a separate book. Because the stems are thicker than single-petal flowers, placing them in a telephone book will cause the pages to remain slightly raised, causing air to enter. As a result, the petals will not remain flat on the pages and will crumble, and all efforts of planting and gathering will be wasted.

When I need to use a heavier stem in a bridal bouquet, I use an X-acto knife to slice the back of the stem to lay it flat on the surface of the picture backing I am using. The stem will have the look of heaviness it needs without being too bulky to be framed correctly. This method is best applied when I design a large picture using large flowers. When the back of the stem is reduced, it is easier to frame.

These flowers were pressed with the stems intact.

Tip:

While designing, if you decide you do not want to use the stem after you pressed it, you can simply cut it off.

Method 2

Use this method if you are going to use certain varieties for a Victorian-type picture (see Chapter 5). Here, it is better to remove the stems and press the quantity of flower heads you need for the round or oval picture frame. The leaves or ferns are first applied, and then only the flower heads. Pansies, Queen Anne's lace, and cosmos are favorites for a Victorian arrangement.

Method 3

The third method is to press only the petals separately. This can be useful when pressing wedding bouquets for framing. Remove the individual petals from the flower head and place them in sequence; you are going to reconstruct the flower with the petals in order (as indicated in the picture). Rose petals, bachelor's buttons, zinnias, and peonies will do well with this method. Carefully remove the petals from the flower head and place the petals on newspaper or in the flower press.

Pressing Multi-Petal Flowers

Place the petals in a circle with the larger petal outward. This will make reassembling easier knowing where each petal fits. You don't need to use all of the petals because the flower will become too bulky to fit into a glass frame (if you are making a picture). Use this method when the flower is still fresh; once the petals are dry, they will crush and cannot be used.

When reconstructing the pressed flower, place the flower's center where you would like it to be (with or without the stem; the stem can be added later if you want it to be in the picture). Start with the largest petals and circle around the center of the flower. Continue doing this until the smaller petals are placed. You don't have to use the entire group of large petals; flowers in a frame should not be too bulky. (When the center of the flower head is too bulky to use in a picture, I sometimes substitute the center of a cosmos because is not as bulky and has the same effect.) Make sure that the petals and leaves are perfectly dry before designing, or the stem and petals will rot.

This shows the sequence in which these petals should be reassembled.

Pressing Flowers With Their Leaves, Pressing Flowers With a Natural-curved Line, and Pressing Fern and Foliage With a Curved Line

A. Nature designs which type of leaf formation will blend with each flower, although voids are necessary depending on your project. If you are designing stationery and adding only one flower, the leaf and flower may be together already (if you kept them on the stem). There are times you might have to remove some of the leaflets so your arrangement has a light, airy feeling. Leaving too many leaves on will cause a heavy look.
B. A natural bend to the stem will give a natural look to any flower line arrangement.
C. Ferns also have a natural bend. Sometimes a curve is natural; other times, you can twist a vine yourself and place it in a telephone book or flower press. It will dry exactly as you placed it.

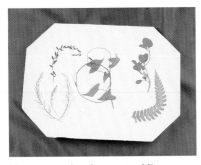

These examples show natural lines.

_____

Tip:

You can curve the flowers, leaves, and stems in any shape when they are being pressed. This will give movement to any design, instead of looking stiff.

Press flowers in different positions. This natural bend creates a flow. When you design using a line arrangement, you will see how it all comes together. Try curving grasses and ferns. Grape vines, as well as other wild vines, have a natural grace.

With some smaller varieties, I try to cut the flowers with the cluster of leaves still attached. This is a good method to use when pressing fruit blossoms or bridal wreath. Make sure that the cluster is not too thick, causing the tiny flowers to stick to each other. If they need to be thinned out, you can do that at this time. I find if the leaves are a graceful cluster after pressing, they can be used "as is" in a picture or for stationery. If some leaves are pruned, do not discard them; they can be used for filling in your arrangement.

Pressing Foreign Plant and Flower Varieties

Foreign countries have different plant and flower varieties that can be fun to press along the way. It is fun to discover a wildflower in an area that you least expected, so press it and see the magical results. What a wonderful memory the flowers will hold for you!

If you decide to press flowers in a foreign country, keep in mind the humidity factor and pick the flowers early in your stay to make sure they have ample time to dry. Press flowers in a telephone book or flower press (use a magazine if you have no other options, but make sure it does not have shiny paper which will not absorb the moisture within the flower). Flowers will do well in a tropical climate only if the room is well air-conditioned. Many tropical hotels do not have air conditioning because there is a cool breeze in the evening; however, when the humidity is high during the day, it will affect the conditioning process. To avoid becoming disappointed and not succeeding in your efforts, place a heavy weight on the magazine or newspaper. Keep the flowers in newspaper as described in Chapter 3 because it is good for packing and then storing upon your return home.

When you are packing to return home, wrap the pressed flowers in newspapers, and tie the bundle securely so that the flowers will not be able to move and be ruined while in transit.

Before packing to take them home, make sure they are in good condition. If so, place them in a paper bag. Do not use a plastic bag, because it will retain moisture like a greenhouse, causing your carefully pressed flowers to rot. Place the package on the bottom of a flat suitcase.

Aboard the flight you will be given a custom declaration to fill out, asking if any plants are being brought into the country. Upon reaching customs, and the declaration reviewed, an agricultural agent will be called. He or she will ask you questions about what kind of plants or flowers you have. He or she may ask you to open the package. I assure them that when I press them they are perfectly dry and that I was careful to see that there were no insects.

Making Potpourri

Have a catch-all, like a box, for petals or flowers you are not using for pressing. Let them air-dry on screening that is slightly raised; air will circulate above and below the petals. Petals also can be placed on newspapers to dry. They should not be dried in direct sunlight, because their colors will fade.

You can also dry the complete flower head. The petals will curl, but that will add charm to the potpourri. You can air-dry small flowers like daisies, bridal wreath, or cosmos. Other flowers that can be used include lavender, lily-of-the valley, honeysuckle, mock orange, stock, and peonies.

An easy way to add a scent to potpourri is to put some of your favorite perfume on a cotton ball and place it in the container that will hold the potpourri.

Use a box with a see-through lid or an interesting shaped bottle to store potpourri. Tie a ribbon around the container and it will be a beautiful gift.

Potpourri can make an elegant statement in any home.

Pressing Flowers from a Special Arrangement

You may want to press flowers that were in an arrangement from a florist. In order to keep a flower arrangement fresh as long as possible, a florist must condition the flowers. This process is done by placing the stems in a bucket of water for several hours; hence they absorb water. This is in opposition to pressing flowers! Whereas in pressing flowers the moisture is removed, the florist adds moisture to the flowers. If flowers retain too much moisture while in the pressing process, they will lose their color and turn brown. Yet, you can press flowers from an arrangement.

If you plan on pressing a floral table arrangement or a bridal bouquet and there are several hours of traveling time, do not put the flower arrangement in a plastic bag. The florist has already conditioned the flowers, and by placing them in a plastic bag, the excessive water that the flowers absorbed will cause the arrangement to rot. In that case, it is better to package the arrangement in a paper bag, but remove it immediately upon reaching your destination.

Be patient, making sure the flowers are dry before you begin to press them. This is a very important step in successful flower pressing. There are no short cuts; if you rush this step, you will not have quality flowers to work with.

(Note: Plants will be confiscated if they are found to contain pests or disease.) I have not had any difficulty with customs when bringing in pressed flowers.

If you know beforehand which plants or seeds you want to take home, request a permit from APHIS (Animal and Plant Health Inspection Service). You can reach it at www.aphis.usda.gov (contact customer service). It will take about one month for APHIS to process the permit. It has a list of acceptable plants that can be brought into the United States. Before you return, there are steps to follow:

1. Make sure the plants are soil-, seed-, and pulp-free. Pack them in a clean container.
2. Label the plants with their Latin names or the accepted English language names. You can label bromides, orchids, ferns, and succulents by these categories only.
3. Indicate the country of origin (and city and province or state if they are from Mexico or Canada) on the label.

Storing Pressed Flowers

This step is as important as it is to pick and press flowers. Make sure flowers are perfectly dry before removing them from telephone books or flower presses. You can check this by picking up the stem; the flower will look stiff and stand upright. There are times that the center of a flower will stick to the paper. If you pull on it, you will damage the flower or petals. You can remove it by using a nail file or the edge of a small pointed knife and gently lift it up.

Some people remove flowers from the newspaper or flower press and put them in labeled boxes. I do not like this method, because if I am looking for a particular size, shape, or color of flower, I do not want to damage any along the way. Because the flowers are brittle, they will break with each search in the box and the flowers will not remain flat. Remember, the flowers are very brittle and should remain in the newspaper. This ensures that they will remain flat and stay in perfect condition until you are ready to use them. It will also prevent moisture from ruining your supply.

I remove and stack pages of each variety. Never remove them from the original newspapers used for pressing. I use large-sized manila envelopes and label each envelope with the name and color of the flower or leaf and place the newspaper within. When you are designing your arrangements, you may need to look for certain colors and varieties, and this is the easiest and the most efficient method to find what you are looking for.

You may discover tiny bugs that seem to appear within the flowers. If this should occur, mothball flakes are a good deterrent. Put a few flakes in each envelope, and the problem should be solved. Another way is to treat a sheet of shelf paper with insecticide and place it in the envelope.

DESIGN TECHNIQUES

Harmonic notes in nature
Music played in color
Purple and pink—blue and gold
Essence of light and dark and
  changing hues
Creating a kaleidoscope of design.

Bernice Wechsler Peitzer

I have always applied flower arrangement techniques when working with pressed flowers, because the principles are basically the same for both; the end result is a good composition that will be pleasing to the eye and have a professional quality. Pressed flower arrangements should not look stiff, dead, or glued; they should look as if they are still growing in your garden.

I had the occasion to watch a Japanese designer create silk flower arrangements. I noticed that the overall designs did not keep with the traditional flower arranging techniques of the Orient discussed later in this chapter. We talked about it, and she felt that as long as the arrangement was pleasing to the eye you can let your imagination soar. The bottom line is to enjoy what you are doing and remember you are the artist.

When constructing a pressed flower arrangement, follow these four basic steps:

1. Select material.

2. Choose sprays and foliage that will determine the main line.

3. Create a center of interest (focal point).

4. Fill additional pressed flowers in to complete the design.

When planning your pressed flower arrangement, it is important to keep in mind what type of line arrangement you will use, accent, balance, the focal point, harmony, rhythm, and scale. All of these points contribute to making a good design. Design consists of the form, shape, and the line of the flower arrangement. Decide which type of form you wish to use, and it becomes the backbone of your arrangement.

Try looking at pictures of flower arrangements for ideas. You can find such pictures in calendars or on greeting cards. You will see different techniques and color combinations that professional flower designers use.

Accent is a sharp contrast in color, size, or form. When used it can first catch the eye and then lead it through the rest of the arrangement.

Balance is needed so the arrangement looks stable, not as if it is going to tumble over. The secret lies in the positioning of the plant material.

Focal point is the center of interest in an arrangement.

Form refers to the type of flowers and foliage you will use.

Harmony requires that the plant material is all "in tune," resulting in a unified whole.

Line means the "direction" of the arrangement, like vertical or horizontal.

Rhythm is the feeling of a natural flow as the eyes view the arrangement.

Scale is the size relationship of the corresponding parts in a composition.

Shape is how the arrangement should look when it is finished.

Different Line Arrangements

Flower arrangements can have various line arrangements. The picture shown below was designed to show the variety of line arrangements that can be used with pressed flower designs. It also shows how to apply flowers in a frame with several openings. Frames with several openings like that shown can be purchased in any craft or frame shop. The next two pages describe the arrangements shown in these openings.

This silver frame has seven different pressed flower arrangements in its openings.

Top left: The **oriental** flower arrangement consists of three levels:

1. The top flower is heaven. This branch is the longest and is placed in the center.
2. The middle branch is man and can be placed on either side.
3. The earth branch is placed in front of the heaven branch.

The key to designing an oriental flower arrangement is simplicity. Leaves, ferns, and grasses are important features in this type of design.

Center left: Victorian arrangements are usually designed in a round or oval frame, which adds charm to the décor of the period:

1. Place foliage on the background.
2. The focal point can either be on the bottom center (as shown) or simply designed in an oval shape.

If you decide to use a Victorian-type arrangement, apply no more than three layers, because you do not want to hide the "underneath" flowers.

This Victorian arrangement was designed to look like a basket. First, I placed the fern, then I added the blue Japanese blossoms. The pink bridal wreath helps the arrangement look as if it is cascading. Finally, I interspersed double purple deutzia and white Queen Anne's lace florets with the rest.

For this Victorian arrangement, I first placed heavy fern in an oval line. Then, I placed many shades of large pink and burgundy cosmos at the base, going upward to add depth to the picture. The lily-of-the-valley and lythrum bring the line upward.

This antique gold frame is perfect for a Victorian arrangement because of its oval opening. I first created an oval with leaves, then added the flowers, beginning with orange Japanese blossoms (they are the largest flowers used). Next, I added purple and lavender larkspur for contrast. The yellow coreopsis verticillata grandiflora brought light into the picture and out of the frame. Finally, I used clusters of white choisya ternata to bring out the colors of the other flowers.

Bottom left: Many types of flower arrangements come in the **crescent** design. This curvy look is charming in a wall hanging.

1. Place either foliage or pointed flowers to form a crescent.
2. Place a flower as the focal point at the center of the joining points.

Top center: The **s-curve** design is an artistic way of designing with flowers.

1. Create an "s" with foliage.
2. The focal point is in the center of the "s"; place a heavy, large flower in the center.
3. Add smaller flowers at either end.

This picture features a horizontal line. The three large orange Japanese blossoms serve as the focal point. On either side, I placed purple fruit blossoms for contrast and then added white clematis recta for lightness. I outlined the entire arrangement with sweet pea tendrils to give it motion.

Top right: Horizontal design. This design is lovely in a grouping for a horizontal wall hanging:

1. Place foliage in a horizontal position.
2. Place a large flower in the center as the focal point.
3. Add any other type of smaller flower.

Bottom right: Right-angle design (which is the focal point of your arrangement):

1. Place the foliage with the heavier density at the angle you desire.
2. Place the largest flower, largest cluster, or darkest color at that angle.
3. Add additional flowers extending from the focal point seeing that the flowers' sizes get smaller as they reach the ends.
4. Add additional foliage if necessary.

Center right: This is the **vertical** design, which is the most common when designing with pressed flowers.

1. Place the central flower in the middle of the working area.
2. Add flowers on either side at different heights. The flowers can be of the same variety or different.
3. Add foliage on either side.

I used a vine to give interesting flow to this vertical arrangement. I placed a large pink and a small purple cosmos as the focal point. At the base, I put a cluster of lavender bridal wreath, and to the left a spray of blue deutzia. At the top, I added a cluster of white choisya ternata to bring the eye upward, so the entire arrangement is pulled together.

One peony petal serves as the focal point of this vertical arrangement. The ferns were placed so that the petal seems to grow out of them. On one side, I added two blue spike wildflowers, two lythrum florets, and a cluster of white choisya ternata. On the other side, I used one purple larkspur, a cluster of white clematis recta, and two blue spike wildflowers for balance.

This vertical arrangement uses one large pink cosmos as the focal point. On either side I added purple deutzia and interspersed blue double deutzia. The white daisy and a cluster of yellow bridal wreath serve as fill-ins. The clusters of white choisya ternata make up the base.

1. Lay a plastic tarp, then a few layers of newspapers, down on your work surface. Also place a few layers of newspaper near your work area. (You will be placing the freshly dyed flowers on the newspaper, and they have a tendency to drip.)

2. Place the foil dish and the plastic container close to each other on the newspapers.

3. Raise the foil dish slightly at one end with the wedge; anywhere between 3/4 to 1 inch will do. (Make sure that the lip of the foil pie tin has enough space so excess dye will not run over onto the paper underneath. When you place the flowers in the foil dish, it must have enough slant for the surplus dye to drain away from the flower heads.)

4. Fill the plastic container half full with water.

5. With the teaspoon, add about a fourth of the amount of dye you intend to use to the container with the water. Mix together.

6. Test the dye with one or two flowers before dyeing all of them. Hold them by the stem and dip them into the dye, immersing only the head in the dye. Some flowers take longer to absorb the dye and can be left in the container with the stems out.

7. Place them in the foil dish and let them drain for a few minutes. If you are satisfied with the color, continue with the rest of the flowers.

8. If you find that the color is too light, add more dye, but if the color is too strong, add more water. Remember, you can always add more water or dye if needed.

9. Some flowers, like the alyssum and fruit flowers, have shorter stems. In order not to put your hands in the dye, place the flower heads in the dye and let them stay there for a few minutes. With the fork or spoon with holes, scoop them out and place them in the foil dish to drain.

10. When you are satisfied that enough of the dye has drained, with the fork or spoon, transfer the flowers to the newspaper. It doesn't matter whether the flower heads are faced up or down; the newspaper will absorb the remaining moisture.

11. If you are dyeing many flowers at one time, the newspaper will have to be changed frequently; it is not good for any flowers that are eventually going to be pressed to stay in a moist environment for an extended time. Let flowers dry completely.

13. If they feel dry to the touch, you can press them. If they are pressed before their time, during the process of pressing, they will stick to the newspaper and the petals will break when you try to remove them.

14. When the excess dye has accumulated in the foil dish, gently pour it into the wide mouth container of that particular color to reuse. After the dyeing process is completed, cover the plastic container for use at another time. If you find that over time the dye has crystallized, just add water and it can be used again.

You will need

Plastic tarp
Newspaper
Tin foil pie dish
Plastic container with a
    wide mouth
Wedge
Teaspoon
Several colors of water-
    soluble dyes (powder
    or liquid)
Latex gloves
Fork or spoon with holes

Method 2

You may find that either after pressing flowers, or after a long duration of storage, the petals have lost some of their color. This is the perfect way to perk the color up!

1. Cover your work area with a few layers of newspaper. Make sure that the flower heads are upright. Leave the flowers on the newspaper used to press them.

2. Dip the paintbrush into the dye (see the previous page for mixing instructions). Remove excess dye on the brush by gently stroking the brush against the container's side. Make sure that the dye does not drip.

3. Gently place your finger in the center, holding the flower firmly.

4. Dip the paintbrush into the dye and gently paint the petals, going from the center of the flower to the tips of the petals.

5. After all of the flowers have been dyed on that page, place the page in an area to dry (because moisture is being added to the petals). Watch to make sure the petals don't curl. If this begins to happen, you know that the petals are drying. Cover them with the newspaper and again place them into a telephone book or flower press.

6. The drying time is approximately five days; after that they are ready for use.

There is a spray on the market called Just For Flowers that can be purchased in most craft stores (see Resources). Just For Flowers is not water-soluble and is good to use on flowers for some stationery projects because the colors will not run onto the paper (while water-soluble dyes will run). I do recommend this spray when you want to color a small amount of flowers after they are completely dry and pressed. The colors are translucent and do very well on white flowers. Make sure to follow the manufacturer's directions when using this product.

ℙROJECTS

Not only is it a joy to pick and press flowers and foliage, but it is also fun to create one-of-a-kind projects using different methods and unexpected treasures found around your home, including shells, leftover tiles, lenses from eyeglasses, discarded shingles, and perfume or spice bottles. As you go here or there, you will see objects that can be used when designing with pressed flowers. As long as the working surface is flat or slightly curved, anything can be used. Both children and adults will enjoy making many of these projects to display their creativity.

Through the years, new ideas have come to me, and one idea usually leads to another. It is always a pleasant challenge to develop projects into an attractive, professional-looking gift that I am proud to give to friends and relatives—and even sell. I have found it is stimulating to start a new project, and even more exciting when it reaches the retail market.

You should have clear sailing ahead with any of these projects; all obstacles have been worked out. All you need to do is have fun and not be afraid to experiment.

Joy is spiritual and spirituality is sharing your love. God is singing through the birds calling me to come.

Bernice Wechsler Peitzer

Notes for All Projects:

❈ You will need assorted pressed flowers and foliage for all projects. Many of the flowers used in the samples are listed in Chapter 1; also see Chapter 5 for a listing of flowers that work well together.

❈ Choose your design and read through all directions before beginning your project.

❈ Try drawing your design on paper before applying it to your project.

❈ Dyed flowers can be used for all projects. If using dyed flowers, spray them with Krylon No. 0500 before applying Mod Podge. This will prevent the dye from running onto the project's surface.

❈ Refer to Chapter 5 for design ideas and strategies.

❈ You can use any line arrangement discussed in Chapter 5 for any project.

❈ You can sign your work with Black Magic India Ink for Film before you cover the project's surface with Mod Podge or Krylon triple-thick crystal clear glaze No. 0500, depending on the project. It is waterproof, so when you apply Mod Podge or Krylon, the ink will not rub off or run. (I have signed most of the samples shown in this chapter.)

❈ If you find that some of the leaves or petals have lifted after you apply your design, take a small paintbrush and apply glue or Mod Podge (depending on what you used) under them and press gently to adhere them.

❈ After adhering the flowers and foliage to the project's surface, make sure they lie flat; if they don't, they will eventually break off.

❈ If glue or Mod Podge runs onto the projects surface, blot it gently with a damp cloth (if it is a non-paper surface) and then with a white tissue, or with just a white tissue.

Mod Podge

For many projects, you can apply Mod Podge with a sponge brush.

Mod Podge is the original all-in-one sealer, glue, and finish (matte or glossy) that can be used with nearly all pressed flower projects. It is perfect for use on wood, paper, fabric, glass, and other porous surfaces. It is a waterproof formula and is fast drying. It is a simple and easy way to protect your designs and makes it possible to choose a larger variety of objects, shapes, and surfaces to work on.

When using a flat brush, Mod Podge has a tendency to leave streaks. This can be avoided by either using a sponge brush, or just smooth it out with your finger. I sometimes dip a paintbrush in water (not too much) and go over the surface of my project to eliminate streaks.

Although I like to use Mod Podge best of all, there are other coatings, like Enviro-Tex Lite, on the market that can be used, but they are very tricky because temperature and humidity must be closely monitored. Krylon triple-thick crystal-clear glaze No. 0500 can be used to spray on flowers used on pendants, pins, bottles, and any other glass surface. Read and follow the directions very carefully before using this product.

Using Mod Podge With Dyed Flowers

Before applying Mod Podge, I spray the flowers lightly with hair spray (do not use a hair spray that has a yellow tint). A clear lacquer, like Krylon, can also be used. Let dry and spray again. This will prevent the colored dye from bleeding onto your background. It is important that you spray the flowers; if you don't, the colors will run.

Other Adhesives

You will need a good-quality glue when making jewelry (for attaching pins, etc.). I particularly like to use Bond 527, which is super strong, clear drying, durable, and flexible. For many projects in this chapter, Elmer's glue works well for gluing flowers to the project surface.

JEWELRY

Jewelry is fun to make for yourself or to give as a unique gift. Your creativity will bring many admirers! I have included jewelry made with jewelry castings, eyeglass lenses, crystals, tile, onyx, wood, and watch cases so you can make attractive pins, bracelets, and pendants.

Project List

Project

Jewelry and Magnets Using a Jewelry Casting

Tip:

If you are making a pin, make sure that the back of the object has ample space to glue it on. When gluing on a pin, make sure that the pin head is in the center. A common mistake is to leave it in the downward position, causing it to stick when the glue is applied. Check the pin within twenty minutes to see that it has not shifted. If it has, adjust it in the right position.

Using a Bale: *If you are going to use an object as a pendant instead of a pin, purchase a bale, which will come flat. The most common and inexpensive variety is a leaf design that comes in two sizes. Place a pencil in the middle of the bale and gently squeeze to create a curve, which will fit any curved surface.*

You will need

Flowers and foliage
Porcelain or heavy white
    paper
Pencil
Scissors
White glue (in dish)
Cocktail toothpick
Jewelry casting
Mod Podge and paint-
    brush or Krylon
Pin back, bale and chain,
    or magnet
Bond 527

*From the left: The **square pendant** was designed on a white paper background. I used purple and pink bridal wreath, pink choisya ternata, and Queen Anne's lace. The **round pendant** at top was designed on glass. It uses an orange cosmos, yellow Queen Anne's lace, and a touch of small pink buds. The **small oval pin** has a cluster of choisya ternata on a white paper background.*

Jewelry castings can be used for pins and pendants; some come with a loop to be worn as either. A porcelain disk can be purchased separately. When buying jewelry castings, ask for a discarded disk of the same size to be used as a pattern when cutting your paper background.

When designing on a small surface, you will find it is best to take some flower clusters apart and use a smaller individual flower such as bridal wreath, small daisies, larkspur, or individual small petals. Use one or three small flowers rather than the cluster. Tiny petals from the bachelor's button could be taken apart and used as a spike flower or small bud.

1. If you are using paper for the background instead of a porcelain disk, use the extra disk to trace a pattern on the paper. Cut the paper for the background evenly because any nicks or uneven cuts will show.

2. Apply white glue to the ridge of the casting. Gently press the paper in place.

3. Apply glue to the backs of the flowers and foliage with the toothpick. Press the flowers onto the background so they remain flat.

4. Apply Mod Podge with the paintbrush or Krylon to the project's entire surface. Let dry completely.

5. Attach the bale to the top or the pin or magnet to the back of the project with Bond 527. If making a pendant, put the chain through the bale.

Project **Magnets and Pins**

Clockwise, from the top: The **small oval metal casting** *has one pink deutzia. The* **square picture** *uses a cluster of orange bridal wreath and scattered white choisya ternata. The* **oval porcelain** *has a lavender fruit blossom with a cluster of orange choisya ternata. The* **brown octagon frame** *features a Johnny-jump-up with a cluster of bridal wreath buds.*

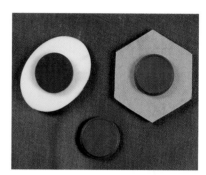

Magnets can easily be applied to your project using Bond 527.

Create a miniature arrangement for your refrigerator or a beautiful pin using different sized and shaped objects. If making a magnet, do not use a roll of magnetic tape, because it is not strong enough to hold the metal castings (the same as those used for jewelry; see the pervious page). A 3/4-inch diameter round disk will hold the metal casting; it is super-strong and will not cause your project to slide or fall from any surface.

1. Apply glue to the backs of the flowers and foliage with the toothpick. Attach them to the tile or casting, making sure they remain flat.

2. Apply Mod Podge with the paintbrush or Krylon to the project's entire surface.

3. Optional: If you are using a jewelry casting and you want to make a miniature picture frame, cut clear acetate instead of glass to the size needed for your frame. Frame, as indicated on page 98.

4. Attach the magnet or pin to the back of the project with Bond 527.

Note: Try using miniature flowers for this project.

You will need

Flowers and foliage
White glue (in dish)
Cocktail toothpick
Small square or rectangular piece of floor tile or the same type of casting used for jewelry
Mod Podge and paintbrush or Krylon
Optional: Clear acetate and other framing materials (see page 91)
Scissors
Round magnet or pin back
Bond 527

Project

Pins and Pendants Using Eyeglass Lenses

*The **oval pin** on the left has miniature pink roses and an orange choisya ternata. The **pendant** on the right features a deep purple cosmos, orange wildflower, one light pink bridal wreath floret, and one orange choisya ternata.*

You will need

Flowers and foliage
Lens
Ammonia and water or
    window cleaner
Paper towel
White glue (in dish)
Cocktail toothpick
Krylon
Two-hole pin back or bale
    and chain
Bond 527

Discarded eyeglass lenses work great as pins or pendants. If you do not have any old lenses, check your local eyeglass establishment for discarded lenses. Do not use a lens with a bifocal line, because it will show and distract from your flower design.

When working with glass, keep in mind that you may have to attach a pin to the back (if you are making a pin). Use a larger flower or leaf in that area so the mechanics of the pin will not be seen.

1. Wash the glass with ammonia and water or window cleaner. Dry completely with the paper towel.

2. Apply glue to the backs of the flowers and foliage with the toothpick. Attach them to the front of the lens.

3. Apply Krylon to the project's surface. Let dry thoroughly.

4. Glue the pin on the back of the lens or attach the bale to the top with Bond 527. If making a pendant, put the chain through the bale.

Tile Pins and Magnets

Clockwise, from the top: The **large square** *has yellow coreopsis verticillata grandiflora, choisya ternata, and deutzia buds. The* **vertical rectangle** *tile uses bridal wreath florets. The* **small square** *has two choisya ternata florets. The* **horizontal rectangle** *pin uses deutzia and choisya ternata.*

Small squares or rectangles of discarded bathroom tile can be used as pins or with a magnet to bring flowers indoors. They are small and delicate and can add beauty to any outfit or your home.

1. Clean the tile's surface with soapy water. Dry completely with the paper towel.

2. Apply glue to the backs of the flowers and foliage with the toothpick. Firmly press onto the tile.

3. When the arrangement is completely dry, cover the project's entire surface with either Mod Podge with the paintbrush or Krylon. Let dry completely. Repeat twice.

4. When the piece is completely dry, turn the tile over and glue on the magnet or pin back with Bond 527.

You will need

Flowers and foliage
Square or rectangular piece of tile
Soapy water
Paper towel
White glue (in dish)
Cocktail toothpick
Mod Podge and paintbrush or Krylon
Magnet or pin back
Bond 527

Project

Pendant, Pin, and Bracelet Watches

*Clockwise, from the top: The **pin** was designed by first pasting a paper backing on the back of the watch and then applying a small cluster of pink choisya ternata. Because the working area of the **pendant** was so small, I used one purple bridal wreath floret with a leaf on either side. The **bracelet**'s working area was larger, so I designed a cluster of pink bridal wreath and blue, white, and purple choisya ternata. The bridal wreath floret was not glued completely, which caused the flower to raise, adding another dimension and interest to the design (usually I do not recommend this, but it added a charming effect to this piece).*

You will need

Flowers and foliage

Small screwdriver

Watch case

White paper

Scissors

White glue (in dish)

Cocktail toothpick

Pin back and Bond 527 (if making pin)

Jump rings and chain (if making pendant)

Broken watches are often forgotten when placed in the back of a drawer—now you can find a constructive use for them! If the band is in good condition, you can make a bracelet, or you can just make a pin with the case. If you find a watch case where the band is held by a curved loop, add a chain and jump rings for a pendant.

Bridal wreath, with its small flowers, works well. Dyeing bridal wreath will give you many colors to choose from. Use delicate ferns with your flowers. If the case is very small, you can design using one small flower and a small leaf. The trick is to make sure that the case is adequate for the type of arrangement you want.

1. Using the small screwdriver, open the watch and remove all of the workings from the back. Keep the original glass in the watch case; it will hold the flower arrangement in place.

2. Use the watch mechanism as a pattern to cut a small piece of paper that will be a backing for your arrangement.

3. Cut the paper to fit on top of the watch mechanism and glue it together; this will ensure a tight fit.

4. Apply glue to the backs of the flowers and foliage with the toothpick. Firmly press onto the paper background.

5. When completely dry, put the watch back together.

6. If you are making a pendant, attach a jump ring to the area that held the band, and then another (this one ensures the watch will lay flat). Attach the chain. If making a pin, glue it to the back of the watch with Bond 527.

Project Initial Pins

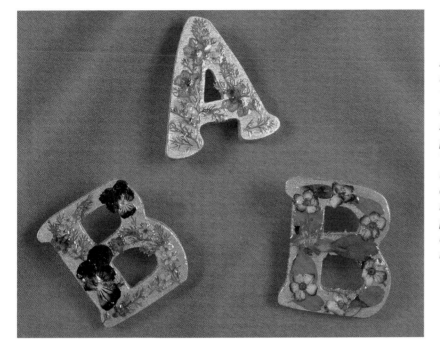

From the left: The first "B" has Johnny-jump-ups and white and orange choisya ternata. The larger flower on the bottom and the lighter flower on the top are surrounded by small flowers. The leaves and flowers were placed so that they created a natural curve. The "A" pin has pink bridal wreath and white choisya ternata. There is an odd amount of bridal wreath, with the larger flower on the bottom. The other "B" uses pink deutzia at center right, with purple bridal wreath florets all around. The leaves form the curve.

This is a fun project to make, and many people love wearing their initial as jewelry. Wooden initials can be purchased in any craft shop. Small flowers or individual petals can be used for this project, and use leaves when working with curves.

1. Sand the edges of the initial with the sandpaper so they are smooth.

2. Put newspaper on a flat surface. Place the wooden initial wrong side up and spray with the gold or silver paint. Spray the sides. When dry, turn the initial right side up and spray, double-checking that all areas are painted. Let dry completely.

3. With a small amount of glue, using the toothpick, place a small leaf so it bends slightly with the curve of the letter (if applicable). You can either cover the entire surface with leaves or reserve areas where the painted spaces will show. Fill in with flowers.

4. After the glue is completely dry, apply Mod Podge with the paintbrush or spray on Krylon. Cover the project's entire surface. When completely dry, repeat twice. Let the initial lie flat to dry completely.

5. Turn the initial over and, using the Bond 527, affix the pin. Make sure that the pin head is upright so it is not glued closed.

You will need

Flowers and foliage
Sandpaper
Wooden initial
Newspaper
White glue (in dish)
Cocktail toothpick
Gold or silver spray paint
Mod Podge and paintbrush or Krylon
Pin back
Bond 527

Mussel Shells and Coral Pins and Pendants

Clockwise, beginning with the coral at top center: This **large oval pin** *has a pink fruit blossom and purple choisya ternata buds. Notice how the flowers fit into the coral's grooves. The first* **mussel shell pendant** *has three pink clematis recta with clusters of white and purple choisya ternata. The second* **mussel shell pendant** *was designed with three pink deutzia, a cluster of white choisya ternata, and was embellished with a tiny pearl. The* **small coral pin** *has one pink deutzia and purple choisya ternata. The* **mussel shell pin** *has a horizontal design (see page 54). I used a pink cosmos, small Lythrum flowers, and one white and blue bridal wreath floret.*

Note: Sketch a design on a piece of paper that lends itself to the shape of the shell or coral.

You will need

Flowers and foliage
Mussel shell or coral
White glue (in dish)
Cocktail toothpick
Mod Podge and paintbrush or Krylon
Pin back or bale and chain
Bond 527

It is fun to walk along the beach looking for shells and coral. They can be used "as is" for jewelry or broken into smaller pieces for embellishment within pictures (see page 95). I prefer mussel or clam shells that have a rainbow inside, and I look for interesting shapes of shells and coral when I make pins and pendants. Decorative paperweights can even be made from larger shells (see page 82).

After gathering shells and coral, put them in a bucket of water and add a quarter cup of bleach. This will dissolve any unwanted material that has attached itself to the objects. Leave them for one day; then remove them, rise well, and dry. Rub the inside of mussel shells briskly to brighten the rainbow colors.

1. Make sure the mussel shell or coral are clean.

2. Apply glue to the backs of the flowers and foliage with the toothpick. Press onto the shell or coral.

3. Apply Mod Podge with the paintbrush or Krylon to the project's entire surface. Let dry completely.

4. If making a pin, glue the pin back onto the back of the piece with Bond 527. If making a pendant, glue the bale to the top of the piece with Bond 527. Attach the chain.

$\mathscr{P}$roject *Sea Glass Pins*

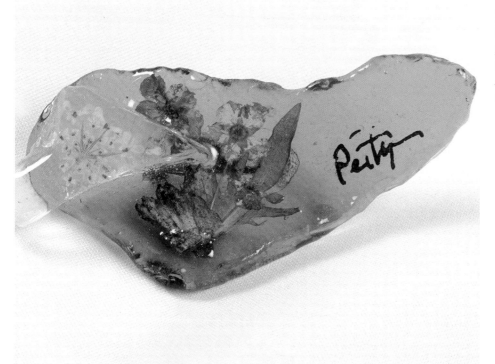

*This **sea glass pin** uses orange bridal wreath on the green sea glass for contrast. One blue deutzia and white Queen Anne's lace were used on the white part.*

Looking for sea glass—broken pieces of glass that have been smoothed by the ocean's motion—is another fun adventure. It is found at low-tide along the beach and comes in different sizes and shapes. (Be aware that some edges may be sharp—use caution when choosing glass for this project!)

1. Wash the sea glass with soapy water. Dry completely with the paper towel.

2. Arrange a couple pieces of glass in a creative design and glue together with Bond 527.

3. Apply glue to the backs of the flowers and foliage with the toothpick. Press onto the glass, making sure that they lie flat.

4. Apply Mod Podge only on the flowers with the paintbrush, or spray Krylon on the entire piece. Repeat. Let dry.

5. Attach the pin to the back of the piece with Bond 527.

You will need

Flowers and foliage
Three to four pieces of sea glass (depending on the size of the glass)
Soapy water
Paper towel
Bond 527
White glue (in dish)
Cocktail toothpick
Mod Podge and paintbrush or Krylon
Pin back

Project

Shell Pins and Decorations

*The **small oval shell** on the left has a dark burgundy cosmos as the focal point, along with three blue lobelia and clusters of orange choisya ternata for balance. The **baking shell** at top features a watercolor wash on the background (see page 93). It has three purple fruit blossoms, three scattered pink bridal wreath florets, and two Queen Anne's lace florets.*

You will need

Flowers and foliage
Mod Podge
Paintbrush
Shell
Pin back and Bond 527 (if making pin)

Small shells—1-1/2 to 2 inches wide—can be used for one-of-a-kind pins. Larger baker's shells, like the kind gourmet chefs use for Coguil St. Jacqu, make great decorative pieces. If you want the piece to stand on its own, purchase a small tabletop easel.

1. Apply Mod Podge to the backs of the flowers and foliage with the paintbrush. Place them on the shell. Let dry completely.

2. Cover just the flowers with Mod Podge. Gently press to keep the flowers flat. Note that the shell's background will yellow slightly if you use too much Mod Podge. Let dry completely.

3. If making a pin, glue the pin to the back of the shell with Bond 527.

Project Crystal Pendants

*For the **pendant** at left, I used blue deutzia and pink bridal wreath. The **pendant** in the middle has pink deutzia and purple bridal wreath. For the **pendant** on the right, I used yellow coreopsis verticillata grandiflora.*

One of the joys of working with crystals is that you can see the flowers from the opposite side. The color of clothing the wearer has on will be the background color of the crystal; it is a charming effect. Look for crystals from chandeliers at lighting fixture stores and even at flea markets.

1. Wash the crystal with soapy water. Dry completely with the paper towel.

2. Attach the bale to the crystal with Bond 527, if it does not have a wire loop.

3. Apply glue to the backs of the flowers and foliage with the toothpick. Place them firmly on the front of the crystal.

4. Spray lightly with Krylon. Let dry completely and repeat twice. Put the chain through the bale or wire.

You will need

Flowers and foliage
Crystal
Soapy water
Paper towel
Bale (see Step 2)
Bond 527
White glue (in dish)
Cocktail toothpick
Krylon
Chain

Project

Onyx Jewelry

*From the left: The **ring** has yellow core-opsis with one orange bridal wreath floret and one bachelor's button petal. The **vertical pin** uses helenium autumnale "coppelia." The **horizontal pin** features Queen Anne's lace and an orange deutzia bud.*

Tip:

Worry stones work great for this project.

You will need

Flowers and foliage
Piece of onyx
Damp cloth
Paper towel
White glue (in dish)
Cocktail toothpick
Mod Podge and paint-
    brush or Krylon
Pin or bale and chain
Bond 527

Onyx comes in a nice variety of shapes, including vertical, heart, oval, diamond, and tear. Many designs and variations can be developed to create a lovely effect.

Try to use light-colored onyx for this project. Also, it is best to work on a medium thickness rather than a very thin or heavy thickness of onyx; a thin piece will break easily, and a heavy piece is difficult to wear.

1. Clean the onyx with the damp cloth. Dry with the paper towel.

2. Apply glue to the backs of the flowers and foliage with the toothpick. Place them on the onyx.

3. Apply Mod Podge using the paintbrush or Krylon to the project's surface.

4. Glue the pin on the back of the onyx or the bale to the top with Bond 527. If making a pendant, put the chain through the bale.

*P*roject *Combs*

For this **comb**, *I used a miniature rose with choisya ternata on either side.*

Flowers designed on combs can be a delicate touch in your hair. It is a great gift for wedding attendants! Use a comb with a 1-1/2 inch border on top (either with a straight or scalloped edge). Horizontal designs (see page 54), as well as a scattering of flowers (an abstract design), look graceful.

1. Clean the comb's surface with soapy water. Dry completely with the paper towel.

2. Apply glue to the backs of the flowers and foliage with the toothpick. Firmly press onto the front of the comb.

3. When the arrangement is completely dry, cover the top area of the comb using either Mod Podge with the paintbrush or Krylon.

You will need

Flowers and foliage
Comb
Soapy water
Paper towel
White glue (in dish)
Cocktail toothpick
Mod Podge and paint-
    brush or Krylon

Giftware

This section includes fun, functional projects you can give as unique gifts or keep for yourself to beautify your living space, including bottles, key rings, coasters, and candles. You will be delighted by the wide range of surfaces—like wood and glass—you can design on.

PROJECT LIST

Project — PERFUME AND SPICE BOTTLES

*From the left: The **jar with the tassel** has a design with three orange deutzia, three blue bridal wreath florets, and two clusters of white choisya ternata. For the **perfume bottle with the red cap**, I used a spray of miniature red roses as the focal point. To the right of the focal point are three blue bridal wreath florets, and to the left are three purple choisya ternata florets. The **small perfume bottle with the gold cap** has small pink deutzia and a cluster of purple choisya ternata for a vertical design (see page 54). The **larger bottle with the gold cap** has one purple bridal wreath floret, an orange wildflower for added height, and three pink choisya ternata florets. For the **tall bottle**, I used a simple design of three blue deutzia and one red choisya ternata floret. The **oval bottle** features one blue deutzia and one deutzia bud. I fanned the design by applying one spray of greenery, two pink and one orange choisya ternata, and one white wildflower spray.*

I love rummaging through flea markets and antique shops, in search of old and unusual bottles.

Remove labels from your bottles before applying your design. Simply soak the bottle in warm water and the label will easily peel off. If you use a bottle that has a label printed on the surface, your flower arrangement should be designed to cover it. A horizontal flower arrangement (see page 54) could be used at this time.

After collecting a number of bottles, make a solution of ammonia and water (approximately two capfuls of ammonia per glass of water). Remove the caps and place the bottles in the solution. Let them soak for a few hours to remove any ingredients or dirt—the bottle will sparkle!

1. Remove the cap from the bottle.

2. Clean the bottle, as described above, and let them dry completely.

3. Apply glue to the backs of the flowers and foliage with the toothpick. Firmly press onto the bottle.

4. When the bottle is completely dry, spray with Krylon. Let dry completely and repeat twice.

5. When the surface is completely dry, put the cap back on.

6. Optional: Tie a colorful ribbon around the bottle's neck for an elegant touch.

Tip:

It is easy to work on a flat or slightly rounded surface, because most petals do not bend easily.

You will need

Flowers and foliage
Bottle
White glue (in dish)
Cocktail toothpick
Krylon
Optional: ribbon

FRAMED MIRROR

*For this **dark framed-mirror**, I chose lily-of-the-valley because of its light feeling. Buds of fruit blossoms and white choisya ternata were added, and more lily-of-the-valley helps bring the eye down. Finally, I added three orange blossoms at the base to give the mirror some depth.*

You will need

Flowers and foliage
Mirror with a flat 1-inch (or more) wooden frame
Mod Podge
Sponge brush
Paintbrush

It is a delight to see an attractive mirror in a room. The flowers you choose will enhance any color scheme and brighten wintry days. A flat frame moulding of one or more inches can be decorated with pressed flowers. Your design could cover all or some sides.

1. Apply Mod Podge to the frame's surface with the sponge brush.

2. Apply Mod Podge to the backs of the flowers and foliage with the paintbrush. Place them on the frame.

3. Using the sponge brush, cover the entire surface with Mod Podge. Make sure all of the leaves and flowers are flat and secure. If you used dyed flowers, brush Mod Podge only on the flowers so the dye will not run onto the background.

 **Project** DECORATIVE DISH

*The red fruit blossoms are the main interest in this beautiful **dish**. I added blue deutzia and purple choisya ternata, and the scattered silver fern brings out the dish's silver rim.*

There is no limit to the designs and flowers you can combine to make this project exceptional. Not only is it a beautiful gift, it can be used to serve guests at an unforgettable party. Imagine the comments you'll receive when you display your creativity! Note: After using the dish, clean the inside only with a damp cloth; do not immerse the dish in water.

1. Clean the dish thoroughly with soapy warm water. Dry completely with the paper towel.

2. Take the flowers and foliage and, with the paintbrush, brush Mod Podge gently on the "face" of each flower and the front of the foliage. Place the flowers and foliage on the outside of the dish in the same positions they were in when inside the dish (see Note at right). Make sure that all of the petals and leaves remain flat.

3. Dip the paintbrush into the Mod Podge and cover the flowers and foliage. If any of the petals raise, gently lift the area with an X-acto knife and brush Mod Podge under the petal. Hold it down until it stays.

4. After completely dry, apply two additional coats of Mod Podge on just the flowers and foliage.

Note: All of the designing is done on the outside of the dish, but lay the flowers inside the dish to see if the arrangement is pleasing before using Mod Podge to adhere them.

You will need

Flowers and foliage
Clear glass dish
Soapy water
Paper towel
Mod Podge
Paintbrush
X-acto knife

Project

ORIENTAL GLOBE DISH WITH STAND

*For this unique, decorative **globe dish**, a heart-shaped vine serves as the line. One red rhododendron is a little off-center; to the left are two dark blue columbine. The cluster of white deutzia brings out the blue and red.*

You will need

Flowers and foliage
Oriental globe dish with
    stand
Window cleaner
Paper towel
White glue (in dish)
Cocktail toothpick

This project gives a lovely oriental touch to your home. Any type of flower arrangement will look beautiful. Because there is a glass backing, keep in mind that the stand will show through the glass. This stand will support the dish and hold the second piece of glass. You can purchase this type of dish at oriental specialty stores (it comes with the black band as shown).

1. Clean the two pieces of glass thoroughly with window cleaner and the paper towel.

2. Place the flowers and foliage inside one piece of glass in your chosen design.

3. With the toothpick, place a dab of glue on the back of each flower and leaf, touching the areas where the petals form; do not glue the entire petal because the glue may show.

4. When the design is finished, make sure there are no specks and the glass is perfectly clean. Put the second piece of glass on top of the one with the design. Secure the two pieces together with the black plastic band. In time, you may find that the petals bend toward the glass. This is natural and is a charming effect for this type of design.

Project GLASS COASTERS

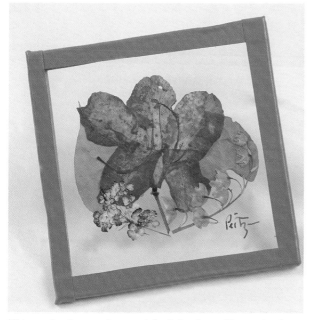

*This **coaster** has one large red rhododendron with a sprig of lily-of-the-valley. To the left is a cluster of blue bridal wreath. I finished the coaster by applying blue tape.*

*This **coaster** has a blue deutzia at left, a daisy in the center, and an orange apple blossom at right. I used gray tape for this sample.*

Pressed flower coasters are charming when placed on a table—they truly bring the outdoors in. What a lovely gift to give yourself!

1. Clean the surface of the glass with the window cleaner and paper towel.

2. Apply a small amount of glue to the backs of the flowers and foliage with the toothpick. Press the flowers onto one of the pieces of glass. When you cover the design with the matching size glass in Step 3, it will secure the flowers. Make sure that the glue is completely dry and there are no specks.

3. Cover the design with the second piece of glass. Place the rubber band around the glass so that it will not slip when placing the plastic tape around the edges. Find the center width of the tape and place it at the edge of the glass. With the felt-tip pen, make small dots around the glass; this is a guide showing where the placement of the tape should be. As you place the tape around the glass, remove the rubber band when you get to that point. Cut the excess.

You will need

Flowers and foliage
Two square pieces of glass
    cut to the same size
Window cleaner
Paper towel
White glue (in dish)
Cocktail toothpick
Rubber band
Plastic tape (color of your
    choice)
Felt-tip black marker
Scissors

Project PAPERWEIGHT

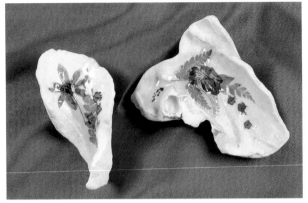

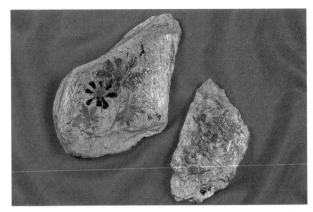

The **small shell** at left has ferns and yellow coreopsis. The cluster of blue bridal wreath on the right brings the arrangement together. For the **larger shell** on the right, I used a fern, with a dark blue Johnny-jump-up in the groove. Three red choisya ternata bring the line upward.

On the **large rock** at left, the two cosmos and three clusters of choisya ternata follow the rock's natural line. The **smaller rock** at right has a spray of red deutzia, a spray of lily-of-the-valley, and a cluster of white choisya ternata.

This **paperweight** has three Johnny-jump-ups and three pink choisya ternata added for interest.

You will need

Flowers and foliage
Glass paperweight, rock, or shell
Scissors
Paper or fabric
White glue (in dish)
Cocktail toothpick
Mod Podge and paintbrush or Krylon

Paperweights, whether made from a regular paperweight form, rocks, shells, are practical and decorative. With the varied shapes of rocks and shells, your design will take on unique forms. Walk along a brook to look for flat rocks, or along the beach for interesting shells. Look for light-colored rocks, like gray or white; lighter tones make a good background color.

1. If you are using a glass paperweight, cut paper or fabric to fit inside.

2. Apply glue to the backs of the flowers and foliage with the toothpick. If using a glass paperweight, affix the flowers and foliage to the paper. If using a rock or shell, glue them directly onto the object's surface. When placing them, make sure all petals lie flat.

3. When you are done designing, and the glue is completely dry, apply either Mod Podge with the paintbrush or Krylon.

4. If using a rock or shell, use the base as a pattern and cut fabric to fit on the underside. Glue fabric to the underside of your project. This will prevent scratching furniture.

Project WOODEN PLAQUES AND KEY RINGS

*The **orange (painted) key ring** at top features two orange cosmos, purple spray of wildflower, and a cluster of white deutzia. The **green (painted) key ring** features one dark orange cosmos, a spray of white deutzia, and one white bridal wreath floret; sprays of coral bell buds are on either side.*

Many craft stores sell wooden products that could be used for wall hangings or key rings. If you are making a key ring, you will need a hole for the chain; either buy a piece of wood with a hole or use a drill to make one. The wood can be left in its natural state or painted.

1. Smooth the edges of the wooden object with sandpaper, if needed.

2. If spray painting the object, place several layers of newspaper on a flat surface. When painting, make sure to cover the outer edges. When completely dry, turn it over and repeat. Make sure that the surface is evenly painted. Let dry completely.

3. Apply glue to the backs of the flowers and foliage with the toothpick. Press them onto the wooden object so they remain flat.

4. When completely dry, apply Mod Podge with the sponge brush, going in one direction, or spray on Krylon. Let dry completely and repeat twice. Note that if using Mod Podge, some streaking may occur. If you do not want streaking, brush the surface with a clean paintbrush and water, or run your finger lightly over the surface to smooth it out.

5. If making a key ring, put the chain through the hole. If making a plaque, attach a sawtooth hanger with the hammer (see page 99).

You will need

Flowers and foliage
Wooden object
Sandpaper
Optional: Spray paint and newspaper
White glue (in dish)
Cocktail toothpick
Mod Podge and sponge brush or Krylon
Optional: Chain (if making key ring)
Sawtooth hanger
Hammer

SHUTTERS

*For this **shutter**, I used two yellow coreopsis verticillata grandiflora on top, with cascading blue fruit blossoms. An orange cosmos is tucked in, which blends with three purple double-petal deutzia and a small cluster of white clematis recta. The lobelia on the right bottom balances the fruit blossoms.*

You will need

Flowers and foliage
Shutter
Paint or varnish of your
    choice
Hook and wire
Paintbrush
Two pieces of Plexiglas cut
    to fit inside of frame*
White glue (in dish)
Cocktail toothpick
Flat head hammer
Brads

Plexiglas should be cut to fit into the shutter frame. You can usually have it cut at the store, or purchase it in large sheets and cut it with a fine-blade saw.

Shutters can make an attractive wall hanging, not only because of the pressed flower arrangement, but also because the wall or wallpaper will be visible as a background for your arrangement. A vertical, horizontal, or abstract design (see pages 54 and 55) can be applied.

Shutters are usually hung in a vertical position, but they can also be hung horizontally. Shutters cannot be hung in windows, a bathroom with high humidity, or walls over a heating vent, because humidity and heat will damage the flowers.

Shutters come in different sizes. Do not purchase window shutters with moveable slots; purchase those that have a central open area suitable for two pieces of Plexiglas. Shutters with a central opening can be found in such stores as Home Depot.

1. Varnish or paint the shutter frame, following the manufacturer's directions.

2. Attach the hook and wire for hanging on the back. It is important to do this step before the project is finished (you do not want to disturb the floral arrangement once it is secured in the shutter).

3. Your work area must be absolutely clean; any specks will find a home on the Plexiglas. If specks gather while you are working, gently blow or brush them away with a dry paintbrush.

4. On a clean surface, remove the covering of one piece of Plexiglas.

5. Make sure the glue is not runny (it shouldn't run on the Plexiglas). Put a small amount of glue on the tip of the toothpick—just enough to hold each flower in place. It is not necessary to glue all of the petals, because the flower arrangement will eventually be sandwiched between the two pieces of Plexiglas.

6. When you are satisfied with your arrangement, make sure there are no remaining specks or spots of dried glue and that the glue is perfectly dry (if not, the glue will find its way onto the other piece of Plexiglas).

7. Remove the protective covering from the second piece of Plexiglas and place it over the flower arrangement. This will keep the flowers in place, and both pieces can be placed in the shutter together. Gently place them in the shutter.

8. With the flat-head hammer, insert brads into the shutter, making sure that the nail heads do not show through the Plexiglas when it faces the front.

Note: Plexiglas comes with a protective covering to prevent scratching.

Project SHINGLES

*The flowers and foliage were arranged around the knots in each of these shingles, which adds to the design. From the left: The first **shingle** has blue fruit blossoms, pink bridal wreath, and a touch of white clematis recta. For the next **shingle**, I used an s-curve arrangement. The foliage was placed first, then the purple Japanese blossom. I then added the orange pointed wildflower and the white choisya ternata and orange fruit blossoms as fillers. The grain of the wood encircles the arrangement of the third **shingle**, with the knot in the center. First, the three purple cosmos were placed, then the blue lobelia, orange fruit blossoms, and finally the white lily-of-the-valley. For the fourth **shingle**, I composed the line with sweet pea foliage, including the tendrils. I then added three orange cosmos, and blue deutzia and light purple wildflowers serve as fill-ins. The final **shingle** has large background leaves in three different positions, along with large red fruit blossoms. The light pink larkspur soften the bright color, and choisya ternata is also present. The grain on the left side of the shingle is too attractive to cover with flowers!*

A shingle wall hanging offers a woodsy look for the right area. For an interesting, arty feeling, select shingles that have an interesting grain or those with knots or round spaces in different parts.

You can use any type of design for your shingle, but vertical (see page 54) and oriental arrangements (see page 53) work particularly well, and depending on where the knots are, and how the grain is running, the crescent (see page 53) or s-curve (see page 53) arrangements could also be used.

Shingles can be purchased at any hardware store or lumber yard. Check for housing construction going on in your area; many interesting shingles are discarded because they are damaged, so ask the builders if you can have them.

1. Notice that there is a thicker part and a thinner part to the shingle; the thicker part should be the top. Examine the shingle and decide which side would be the most attractive for your design.

2. Center and attach a saw tooth hanger 3/4 to 1 inch from the top on the back of the shingle with the hammer. The nail should not penetrate the wood at this thickness.

3. Because shingles are darker than most surfaces you will work with and have a grain, you will need to apply the flowers a little differently. Make sure that the entire backs of the flowers and foliage are completely glued to the shingle. The petals may discolor. If this occurs, glue additional petals of the same flower over the discolored petals. Make sure there are no specks on the shingle.

4. If you used dyed flowers, spray them with Krylon twice. This will also give the wood a nice finish. You can leave it that way or, for undyed flowers, apply Mod Podge with the paintbrush on the flowers only or the entire surface.

You will need

Flowers and foliage
Shingle
Saw tooth bracket and
   nails
Hammer
White glue (in dish)
Cocktail toothpick
Optional: Mod Podge and
   paintbrush or Krylon

𝒫roject CANDLES

*The **votive** at left has Johnny-jump-ups with a tiny pink bud for an accent. The **votive** at right has pink bridal wreath florets and one choisya ternata floret in the center.*

*The **tapers** feature blue and pink bridal wreath, a lavender fruit blossom, and yellow Queen Anne's lace.*

You will need

Flowers and foliage
Mod Podge
Paintbrush
Candle
X-acto knife

Candlelight gives a soft, warm, comfortable feeling to any room. Small, thin, flexible flowers, like like lobelia, bridal wreath florets, and Johnny-jump-ups, work the best on candles' curved surfaces. Individual petals and ferns are also good choices.

1. Apply Mod Podge to the backs of the flowers and foliage with the paintbrush. Place them gently on the candle. Make sure all petals remain flat against the candle.

2. Dip the paintbrush into the Mod Podge and gently cover the surface of the flowers and foliage. Let dry completely. Repeat. If a petal or two has lifted from the candle, gently, using the X-acto knife, lift it and, with the paintbrush, apply additional Mod Podge.

Project GIFT AND KEEPSAKE BOXES

*For the **box** at left, I used four lobelia, two white clematis recta, and one large red fruit blossom; the design "fans out." The **box** at right has lily-of-the-valley and two pink and one lavender larkspur. The ferns develop the line.*

A gift or keepsake box is charming and easy to make. Any type of flower and arrangement can be used. You can give the box as a gift or put a personal treasure inside.

1. Apply Mod Podge to the backs of the flowers and foliage with the paint-brush. Place them firmly on the box's lid.

2. If you used dyed flowers, spray them with Krylon; this will prevent the dye from running onto the lid's surface.

3. Apply Mod Podge with the paintbrush on the flowers only or Krylon to the project's entire surface. Let dry completely. Repeat twice.

You will need

Flowers and foliage
Mod Podge
Paintbrush
White gift box
Optional: Krylon

Project

BISQUE

*The **wall plaque** at left was designed so the flowers are raised (not perfectly flat). This was accomplished by gluing a heavier flower on the surface, then gluing another flower on top of the first, giving it a dimensional look. I used a large white daisy at top, two deep purple larkspur, one yellow coreopsis verticillata grandiflora, and one red fruit blossom; the blue spike wildflower brings the design together. The **oval stand** at right was first covered with rice paper (see page 114), then a watercolor wash was added to highlight the background (see page 93). It features purple larkspur, lily-of-the-valley for height, and three red fruit blossoms. To balance the lily-of-the-valley, I added a white floret of Queen Anne's lace.*

You will need

Flowers and foliage
Mod Podge
Sponge brush
White glue (in dish)
Cocktail toothpick
Paintbrush
Bisque

Bisque is clay pottery that has not been fired. It has a white background and is excellent for working with pressed flowers. It comes in a variety of shapes, including ovals and rectangles, and either has a self-stand or is a wall plaque. Look for bisque at ceramics shops. It lends itself to designing with many types of flower arrangements.

1. Cover the bisque's entire surface with Mod Podge, using a sponge brush. You can use your finger to smooth it out. Let dry completely.

2. Apply glue with the toothpick or Mod Podge with the paintbrush to the backs of the flowers and foliage. Press firmly onto the bisque.

3. Brush Mod Podge only on the flowers with the paintbrush. Let dry completely. Repeat twice.

$\mathcal{P}$ictures

$\mathbf{I}$n this section, you will have the opportunity to create many unique pictures with pressed flowers. The beginning of this section is designed to tell you everything you need to know about putting a picture together, from choosing a backing to applying a design. Then, you will be given options for picture projects, and finally there is information on framing your creation.

PROJECT LIST

CHOOSING A BACKING

Part of the fun of designing pressed flower pictures is selecting the backing or background. There are different types of backings that can be used with pressed flowers; it is up to you to decide on the look you want:

❀ There is a wide variety of colored and shaped **mat boards** currently on the market. The standard is a white or ivory that can be purchased at any craft or art supply store.

❀ **Oriental papers** are nice in contemporary or oriental designs.

❀ **Sumi-e**, an inexpensive soft white rice paper, can be used for backgrounds.

❀ **Gift wrapping or wallpaper** work well, but make sure that the design is muted so it doesn't compete with your flower arrangement.

❀ You can also use **watercolor paper** that lends a heavier texture to the background.

❀ **Fabrics** make attractive backgrounds for many press flower arrangements. **Velvets** make a rich formal appearance, and **burlap and felt** have a more informal look. If you would like more of a formal Victorian look, you can use an **embossed fabric**, which has a busy but interesting effect. Check upholstery shops for obsolete fabric books; many are happy to give them to you, or they might have other scraps of fabric you can use.

*This mat contains seven pictures. I designed a horizontal arrangement in the **elongated oval** at top left, using three orange fruit blossoms and, for contrast, one lavender fruit blossom. In the **rectangle** at bottom left, I used three pink cosmos as the focal point and to the left of them I put two yellow Queen Anne's lace florets. To the right I placed two blue deutzia. In the top center **picture** I wanted a light feeling, so I placed one daisy and one yellow coreopsis verticillata grandiflora to bring height and a feeling of lightness. For contrast, I added lythrum florets and, on the lower part, blue agapathus (Lily of the Nile). The bottom center **circle** has a circular arrangement. After placing the leaves, I added blue fruit blossoms. I then filled it in with white choisya ternata to bring the arrangement together. In the **rectangle** at top right, I placed leaves in a "u" line and added one light pink larkspur, one rose-colored deutzia floret, and a cluster of blue bridal wreath. I used the same leaves I used in the "u" line for the **rectangle** arrangement in the middle on the right side. I added one purple larkspur and a lighter purple fruit blossom. I then added three red choisya ternata florets and one yellow Queen Anne's lace floret. I placed a white bud from a clematis recta pointing upward. In the bottom right **opening**, I placed the leaves in a "u" position and used one large orange cosmos as the focal point. I then added a sprig of lily-of-the-valley and a purple double deutzia.*

Placing a mat in the frame adds a professional quality. Make sure that the mats you purchase are acid-free. You can choose any color, texture, or style to complement your pressed flower picture. You can also use a type of mat that has several openings, resulting in several pictures in one frame. It is a decorative touch for a wall hanging, especially when grouping along with other framed pictures.

GETTING STARTED

Prepare all of your supplies before your start and have a good working area, like a card table, but make sure to cover it with several layers of newspaper.

Supplies and materials needed to frame pressed flower pictures.

1. Select the picture frame. Make sure that the frame is in perfect condition, and that the glass does not have any scratches.

2. If you use a mat board, you do not need to cut a piece of cardboard for the backing. If you use fabric or paper, you need to cut a piece of cardboard the same size as the glass. Use a firm cardboard that doesn't bend. Place the glass on the cardboard or mat board and, with a pencil, trace the pattern. Cut it, making sure that it fits into the groove of the picture frame. If you use a heavier fabric, allow for the extra room by cutting the cardboard slightly smaller. This will allow the heavier fabric to fit comfortably into the frame.

3. If using fabric, after the cardboard is cut, place it on the wrong side of the fabric, allowing the fabric to overlap on all four sides. This must be turned over and held in place with masking tape. When it is securely in place, the corners can be trimmed. This method of securing a fabric background is applicable with square or rectangle frames not larger than a 12 x 14-inch picture size.

Note: When working with large, oval or round frames there is another method that should be used. Masking tape will not hold securely on a larger oval or round frame; the fabric will eventually pucker. Instead of using masking tape, use a needle and heavy thread to sew one side to the other enough times so that the fabric is secured to the cardboard. There is nothing as frustrating as finishing your picture, and after framing, finding that the background fabric is sliding.

You will need

Note: These materials are needed for the backing, applying, and framing stages, presented here and on pages 98 and 99.

White glue (in dish) (I recommend Elmer's all purpose glue or #476A06 Elverette, which is a very thick craft glue that dries clear and flexible and is excellent for gluing pressed flowers and foliage to paper.)
Cocktail toothpick
Small sharp scissors
X-acto knife or nail file
Picture frame and glass to fit
Acid-free mat or fabric (color of your choice)
Backing for the picture itself (which ever you choose)
Square-head hammer
Brads (small nails to hold the picture securely in the frame)
Brown paper backing for frame
Hooks and wire to hang the picture
Masking tape
Needle and thread (if you are using a fabric)
Pencil

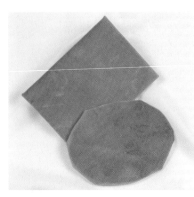

A fabric backing.

The backing at top is taped on, while the oval backing is sewn on.

Note: To test the glue's consistency, dip the toothpick into the cup and, if the glue runs, it is too thin and you should add more glue. Storing glue in a baby food jar is recommended because the glue can be covered tightly when not in use.

APPLYING DESIGNS TO PICTURES

Follow these basic instructions when making a pressed flower picture.

1. It is always best to work within the frame or mat opening. It is an easy way to center the picture. Even if you decide to use a line arrangement, it must be well-balanced within the frame. Be careful not to damage the mat if you are using one. You can cut a mat out of cardboard to the same size, to use temporarily, to keep the final one clean. While working on your design, keep the backing as free from specks as possible. Use the point of a nail file or X-acto knife to gently remove any specks that might appear.

2. Place the backing in the picture frame.

3. Applying the design: Make sure the glue is water soluble, then pour enough for the picture into a dish. The glue tends to harden quickly, so if this occurs, add a little water and mix with the toothpick. Use a thicker consistency when working with some ferns and flowers that are heavy such as dogwood, lily-of-the-valley, lythrum, and zinnia. It is better to use a thin-consistency glue when working with flowers like cosmos, fruit blossoms, poppy, or paper whites. If the consistency is too thin, you will find that the flowers will not stick to the sur face and the glue will run onto the background and damage it. Apply glue to the back of the flowers in the center, gently gluing the base of the petals surrounding the center of the flower; this will prevent the petals from breaking off. Do not glue the entire petal, because this might cause them to pucker on any background. In addition, some flower petals may discolor because of the glue, so it is best not to glue the entire petal. Gently hold the stem, placing the flower in the position of your choice. If the flower does not have a stem, the toothpick with the glue will hold the flower while placing it in the desired position. Should any glue run onto the background, gently blot it with a white tissue.

4. When you are done, you can sign your picture. Typically, this is done in the bottom right corner.

SEAWEED

What a delight it is to walk along the beach in the early morning. I often find seaweed clinging to a rock that is jutting out from the sea or notice another variety floating just under the water's surface. I love to collect seaweed and design pictures I will keep as a remembrance of a joyful vacation. Here are some guidelines for working with seaweed and doing a watercolor wash you will use to make a picture on the next page.

Working with Seaweed

1. Gently grasp the seaweed and place it in a plastic bag.

2. After accumulating all that is needed for your design, put the seaweed in a container of fresh water. (This will remove sand from the seaweed.) Repeat until all of the sand is removed. Note that some sand could be left in for effect when you are designing your picture.

3. Place a few layers of newspaper on a flat surface. Taking one piece of seaweed at a time, place it on the newspaper, forming it in a shape that you can later apply to your project. The seaweed will dry exactly as you placed it.

4. You will notice that the newspaper shows excessive moisture. The paper will need to be changed several times before you press it. When it feels almost dry, it can be placed in the telephone book or flower press; it will take about a week for it to thoroughly dry (see page 46 for pressing directions). Watch the seaweed carefully while the paper is absorbing the excess moisture. Note: Do not allow seaweed to dry so completely that it is too brittle to use.

Watercolor Wash

1. Use clean water to wet the paper.
2. Use a paper towel to absorb any excess moisture from the paper.
3. Apply a color.
4. Use a clean brush to smooth the painting strokes if needed.
5. Layers of color can be added when the first layer is almost dry; allow the colors to blend naturally on the paper.

Hints:

❋ *Two or three colors can be mixed together to produce another color.*
❋ *Adding two or three colors on the brush will give a unique effect.*
❋ *All of the colors must be in harmony with your arrangement.*

Project SEAWEED PICTURE

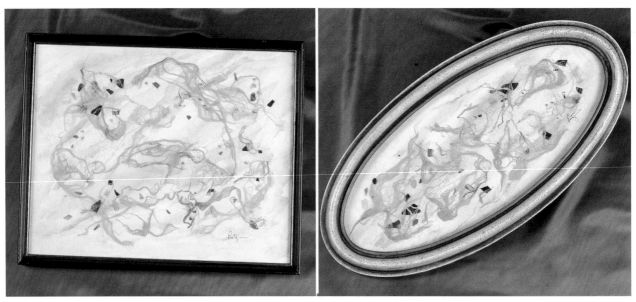

Seaweed pictures *can give the feeling of motion. I applied a green, blue, and yellow watercolor wash depicting underwater color for both of these samples. I added pieces of mussel shell to add interest; these also contribute to the feeling of motion. The off-white elongated oval frame at right was chosen for its weathered look.*

Note: Before starting your project, be sure that the seaweed is perfectly dry.

You will need

Seaweed
Watercolor paper
Watercolor paints
Paintbrush
White glue (in dish)
Cocktail toothpick
Optional: Crushed mother-of-pearl or mussel shells
Materials for framing and backing (see page 91)

1. Follow the directions on the previous page for creating a watercolor wash. Let dry completely.

2. Choose several pieces of seaweed and place them on the paper. Gently lift the seaweed and apply glue to the back of each piece with the toothpick.

3. If desired, glue crushed mother-of-pearl or mussel shells to add another dimension to your picture. (When the picture is framed, the glass will help hold them in place.)

4. Frame the picture (see page 98).

Project WATERCOLOR FLOWERS PICTURE

*For this **arrangement**, I used a spray of pink deutzia in the center, as well as clusters of purple choisya ternata and orange bridal wreath. Because the picture needed a stronger color, I also used three blue watercolor flowers.*

*This crescent line design (see page 53) **picture** has two pink cherry blossoms. Three white Queen Anne's lace florets and clusters of orange bridal wreath are also present. To give the picture depth, I painted blue and purple flowers.*

Painted flowers interspersed with your arrangement is a creative application. Each will add depth to your picture.

When designing with watercolor, decide if you prefer to use complementary colors or hues of the same color. Complementary colors are the colors that are opposite each other on a color wheel (see page 58).

1. Apply glue to the backs of the flowers and foliage with the toothpick. Press them onto the paper. Leave areas for painting flowers.

2. Following the tips below, paint flowers on the paper in the desired areas. Let dry completely.

3. The painted flowers can be outlined with the Micron pen.

4. Frame the picture (see page 98).

You will need
Flowers and foliage
White glue (in dish)
Cocktail toothpick
Watercolor paper
Pencil
Watercolor paint
Paintbrush
Optional: Micron 01 pen
Materials for framing and backing (see page 91)

Tips for Painting Flowers:

❀ *Notice the formation of petals. Some are long and thin, like a daisy, some are wide, like a paper white, some have spikes, like the lythrum, and others have clusters, like the bridal wreath. As you work with flowers you will focus on their blooms, making it easy for you to sketch.*

❀ *Design the pressed flower arrangement on watercolor paper. (You will be painting flowers after you have glued your arrangement on the paper.)*

❀ *Be aware of the spaces where you can place some watercolor flowers. Sketch them with a pencil, making sure their placements are correct.*

❀ *In areas that have pointed, spiky pressed flowers, paint some that are rounded or clustered.*

❀ *When the paint is completely dry, you can outline some or all of the flowers with a Micron 01 pen, which has waterproof black ink.*

Project

WATERCOLOR WASH PICTURE WITH WATERCOLOR FLOWERS

*For this **picture**, first, I applied a watercolor wash of green, blue, and red (see page 93). Then, I placed background leaves, added four cosmos (one burgundy and three deep pink with purple), and one white deutzia. I then placed blue, purple, and pink bridal wreath florets, as well as one orange fruit blossom and a cluster of white choisya ternata. Finally, I sketched and painted flowers to the right to add movement to the design.*

You will need

Flowers and foliage
Watercolor paper
White glue (in dish)
Cocktail toothpick
Materials for watercolor
   wash (see page 93)
Materials for sketching
   and painting flowers
   (see page 95)
Materials for framing and
   backing (see page 91)

This picture uses a watercolor wash as the background, along with watercolor and pressed flowers.

1. Follow the directions on page 93 for making a watercolor wash. Let dry completely.

2. Apply glue to the backs of the flowers and foliage with the toothpick. Press them onto the paper. Leave areas for painting flowers.

3. Sketch and paint flowers (see page 95).

4. Frame the picture (see page 98).

Project FREE-STANDING PICTURE

*The **picture** at left uses a crescent-line design (see page 53) with three orange fruit blossoms and three buds. The line is continued with three purple choisya ternata. For the **picture** at right, I used three pink/purple cosmos; the higher one brings the eye to the poem's first stanza, and the two on the left bring it together. The lavender wildflower brings the eye upward. For the base, I placed three blue deutzia, one lavender fruit blossom, and one Johnny-jump-up. Three clusters of choisya ternata bring out the other colors.*

This is a lovely little treasure; give it in place of a greeting card.

1. Trace the frame backing's outline on the mat board or paper. Cut out.

2. Write or type your message on the mat board or paper.

3. Put a small amount of glue on the mat board's or paper's four corners, using the toothpick. Press down onto the front of the backing so they stay in place.

4. Observe the space around your message to determine the best arrangement. Apply glue to the backs of the flowers and foliage with the toothpick. Press them onto the paper. Let dry completely.

5. Apply Mod Podge to the surface of the flowers and leaves with the paintbrush. Be careful not to get any on the background paper because the Mod Podge will stain it. Let dry. Repeat twice.

You will need

Flowers and foliage
Pencil
Backing from a stand-up frame
Mat board or any other paper
Scissors
Message
White glue (in dish)
Cocktail toothpick
Mod Podge
Paintbrush

When you're done designing a picture, you can frame it. Make sure that the frame is in excellent condition: the joints must fit tightly together, make sure that there are no scratches on it, and if you use an old wooden frame, you may need to refinish it (which you should do before you start designing your picture because it will take three to four hours to dry thoroughly; see the tips at left).

1. Make sure that the picture's background is absolutely clean; there should be no specks on your picture after it is framed. Specks can occur because tiny particles might have been caught within the flowers and foliage. Blowing on the surface very gently will remove smaller specks, but be very careful not to disturb your arrangement. Be aware that the petals will lift if you are not careful when removing specks, so use tweezers.

2. Check the glass to make sure it is clean and free of scratches, the frame is dry, and the glue you used to anchor the arrangement is completely dry (which may take about an hour). If the glue holding the flowers in place is not completely dry, the pressure of the glass on your flower arrangement will cause it to run. If this should occur, the glass must be washed immediately. Be careful when removing the glass that the flower arrangement is not damaged.

3. Place the glass very gently over the front of the picture. Hold the glass firmly in place with both hands while picking up the backing of the picture. You can now see why you needed to use a firm piece of cardboard (to hold the backing). Turn it over and gently place it into the picture frame. Pick the picture frame up while holding it firmly. This is your last inspection to see that there are no specks. Make sure the flower arrangement is exactly as you want it to be; this is your last chance to make any changes.

4. Place the picture frame face down again to secure the picture in place. Use a 5/8-18 size wire brad (nail). This is necessary to ensure that the brad's head does not work through the paper backing. If the brad is too long it will go through the picture frame's moulding. Make sure that the picture and glass are firm and secure. As a rule of thumb, for a 5 x 7-inch frame, I use at least three brads on each of the four sides. Use a square head hammer with gentle pressure to push the brads in place. Do not lean heavily on the glass when you are inserting the brads, because you could break the glass and/or the frame. If you find that you have a lot of framing to do, you can use a professional framing gun with glazing points. The framing goes faster, but you must be careful not to press too heavily or the glass will break. Make sure that the glass and backing have a little room to move.

5. Now put the paper backing on. Brown wrapping paper is perfect and can be purchased by the roll. To back a smaller picture, a brown paper shopping bag can be used. Use either wallpaper or gift wrapping for a pretty backing.

6. Place the picture frame right side up. With a pencil, trace the pattern of the frame on the paper. If you cut the paper a fraction smaller than the pattern you will not have to do any trimming later. Turn the picture frame face down and take a small amount of glue on the edge of an applicator or a toothpick and apply it to the frame. Continue until the entire moulding edge of the frame surface is covered with glue. Do not apply too much glue or it might run in between the side of the frame and the picture. If the glue is too watery it could run onto the glass, damaging your design.

7. Place the paper backing over the moulding of the frame and, with gentle pressure, smooth out any wrinkles. Wait until the glue is thoroughly dry and trim any overlapping paper, if necessary.

Screw and eye hangers and wire.

8. Put in the hooks for hanging the picture. A screw eye hanger or a saw tooth hanger can be used. They come in different sizes, depending on the width of the picture frame moulding. If you decide to use the screw eye hanger, you will need picture frame wire. A heavier weight wire is best for larger pictures or heavier picture frames. To use it, loop the wire through twice and twist securely. This is necessary so the wire does not slip out while the picture is hanging. Saw tooth hangers work well with smaller and lighter pictures.

9. To make the framing complete, cut about 1 inch of masking tape and wrap it around the two ends of the picture frame wire. This gives a professional look.

Saw tooth hanger.

You may want to sign your name on the backing of each picture or use a personalized a rubber stamp for this purpose. If using a stamp, do not press heavily, because it could tear the backing. "Original by _____" looks very professional.

It is advisable to frame your completed picture as soon as possible after completion. This will ensure that your pressed flower picture will remain in place.

MINIATURE PICTURES

The same technique for framing a larger picture can be applied for framing a doll house picture. Cut a piece of backing you will use for the arrangement and use a piece of acetate instead of the glass. Miniature frames are too small to use a hanging implement, so use a glue gun to attach a doll house picture to the wall. By attaching a two-hole pin on the back, it will become a pin (see examples on page 65).

Paper Projects

Paper is one of the most versatile craft mediums around, and now you can learn how to apply pressed flower arrangements to a wide variety of paper items, from bookmarks and photo albums pages to stationery and one-of-a-kind invitations.

PROJECT LIST

Project

BOOK COVERS

Book covers are beautiful and practical—they are great to own or give as a gift. This technique can be used for address, telephone, poetry, or recipe books. There are two options: you can either design an arrangement on paper and apply it to the book, or you can design directly on the book's cover.

Method 1

1. If designing with construction paper, cut it to the size of the book's front cover.

2. Glue the construction paper securely to the book, making sure the four corners lie flat.

3. Apply glue with the toothpick or Mod Podge with the paintbrush to the backs of the flowers and foliage. Place them in the desired positions. Make sure the flowers are completely glued to the surface. Let dry completely.

4. If you are using dyed flowers on construction paper, gently cover just the flowers with Mod Podge, using the paintbrush (this will prevent any dyed flowers from running onto the paper). Let dry completely and repeat twice.

5. With the sponge brush, brush on Mod Podge, going in one direction, over the project's entire surface.

Method 2

1. Apply glue with the toothpick or Mod Podge with the paintbrush to the backs of the flowers and foliage. Place them in the desired positions, directly on the book's cover. Make sure the flowers are completely glued to the surface. Let dry completely.

2. With the sponge brush, brush on Mod Podge, going in one direction, over the project's entire surface.

*The **book** at top left has a white construction paper backing, a bunch of wildflowers that were dyed purple, and one pink larkspur. The **book** at right is on blue construction paper. It features three pink cosmos, a cluster of orange choisya ternata, one white daisy, and one yellow coreopsis verticillata grandiflora. For the **book** at bottom, I designed right on the book's cover. I used orange cosmos, yellow coreopsis verticillata, asparagus fern, and a white spike.*

You will need

Flowers and foliage
Optional: Construction paper
Scissors
Book
White glue (in dish)
Cocktail toothpick
Mod Podge
Paintbrush
Sponge brush

 Project

BOOKMARKS

*From the left: The **bookmark** with the green ribbon has one coreopsis verticillata grandiflora and lily-of-the-valley. The **bookmark** with the white ribbon has three Johnny-jump-ups. The **bookmark** with the purple ribbon has one purple cosmos, one lobelia, and one yellow wildflower.*

Who couldn't use another bookmark? You can be as creative as you'd like, using different colored construction papers and designs, but try a lighter weight flower such as an apple blossom or lobelia.

There are two ways to make bookmarks. With the first, you will seal the bookmark in plastic, and with the second, you will simply cover the flowers with Mod Podge, similar to many of the projects in the book.

You will need

Flowers and foliage
Construction paper
Ruler
Scissors
White glue (in dish)
Cocktail toothpick
Optional: Clear plastic
    sandwich bag, cotton
    pressing cloth, iron
Hole punch
Ribbon, approx. 7 inches
    long
Optional: Heavy book
Optional: Mod Podge and
    paintbrush

Method 1

1. Cut a strip of construction paper 1-1/2 inches wide x 5-3/4 inches long. The paper can be cut into any design.

2. Apply glue to the backs of the flowers and foliage with the toothpick. Press onto the paper. Make sure to leave room at the top for the hole.

3. When the bookmark is completely dry, put it in the sandwich bag. Place the bookmark at the very edge of the plastic bag so it touches the seam on a side and the bottom.

4. Cover the bag with the pressing cloth and press with a hot iron. Do not move the iron in different directions; hold it and press down so the plastic will adhere to the bookmark (count to ten and check).

5. Punch a hole at the top of the bookmark. Put the ribbon through the hole and knot.

6. If the bookmark does not lie flat, put it between two pieces of waxed paper and place it between the pages of a heavy book overnight.

Method 2

Instead of putting the bookmark in a plastic bag in Steps 3 and 4, simply coat the entire surface with Mod Podge using the paintbrush. Follow Steps 5 and 6.

MY JOT-DOWN BOOK

*My **jot-down book** has an informal look, achieved with Johnny-jump-ups and leaves.*

This is a handy little book to take along for quick notes or to give as a favor at a party. It is quick and easy to make.

For this project I prefer to use just leaves and flower heads, which is most practical and will stay in better condition longer than using flowers with stems. With the turning of the pages, there will be less damage to your design.

1. Fold the paper bag or construction paper in half (to 2-1/2 x 5-1/2 inches); this is the cover. With the hole punch, punch two holes on top, 3/4 inch from the fold. Apply reinforcement rings on the inside of the paper.

2. Place the writing paper inside the cover. Center the paper within the cover and, with the pencil, mark inside the two holes. This will ensure that the paper and the cover holes will line up correctly. Punch in the area indicated by the pencil marks.

3. Put ribbon through the two holes and tie in a bow.

4. Apply glue with the toothpick or Mod Podge with the paintbrush to the backs of the flowers and foliage. Press them onto the cover.

5. When the flowers and leaves are dry, carefully cover them, or the entire cover, with Mod Podge and the sponge brush (covering the entire cover will cause the paper to become heavy).

You will need

Flowers and foliage
5 x 11-inch piece of brown paper bag or construction paper
Hole punch
Four reinforcement rings
Six sheets of 4 x 10-inch white writing paper
Pencil
Ribbon
White glue (in dish)
Cocktail toothpick
Mod Podge
Paintbrush
Sponge brush

PHOTO ALBUMS

*For the top **photo** on this page, I used white clematis recta flowers to make the picture stand out. The ferns going upward bring attention to the picture. On the lower **photo**, pink larkspur brings out the flowers in the dress. White larkspur balances the two pictures and brings a light, airy feeling to the page. The pink spike flowers seem to embrace the picture.*

There is no need for a photo album to be boring. Enhancing your favorite photographs with flowers and foliage will add interest and beauty to your cherished memories.

Save some of your favorite sayings from greeting cards you receive. They can express whatever you wish and complement any page, incorporated with pictures and flowers. Notice the use of flowers and a greeting card message on the pink album page on the opposite page. Some greeting cards have a message within an embossed frame. You can cut out the message and use it as a mat for a photograph. With every design, flower, or accessory you use, keep in mind that the end result should be pleasing to the eye.

There are several types of photograph albums on the market. Make sure all materials used when working with photographs are acid free!

When making album pages, I usually use either black or white, although any color can be used. A black background has a dramatic look. Naturally, when using a black background, use white or light-colored flowers that will stand out. When using any regular non-sticky paper, brush several coats of Mod Podge on the flowers and foliage to ensure they will be secure. You can use any color background to fit your album or a white sticky background with any type of covering as long as you make sure the paper and the poly-vinyl covering are acid free. Your photographs will not be damaged and you, your family, and friends will enjoy your decorative photo albums.

White background pages with a plastic overlay are made to be sticky so that when a picture is placed, it will stay exactly where you want it. This type of photo album can be used, but it can be a little difficult, because every little speck that falls will find a home on the page. Therefore, it is very important to keep your work area clean. If specks should appear, gently lift them off with the point of an X-acto knife. The plus side of using this type of photograph album is that your flower designs will be protected and remain in place for a long time without being damaged; no other glue is needed.

Remove the top plastic and place sandwich paper between the cover. This will keep the inside of the plastic clean until your picture and flower design are complete.

Remember you are using flowers that were stored in newspaper. Without realizing it, you may get some of the black print on your hands. If this occurs, wash your hands immediately. If the black print finds its way to the sticky background paper, it is impossible to remove. If this occurs, you will either need to discard the page or try to design over it.

For all types of photo album pages, if the design is abstract (see page 55), use a heaviness of feeling toward the bottom of the page and a lightness toward the top.

Project

General Directions for Decorating an Album Page

1. Glue the photograph to the album paper in the position of your choice.

2. Apply Mod Podge to the backs of the flowers and foliage with the paintbrush, using gentle strokes. Let dry completely. Apply two additional coats of Mod Podge over the flowers only. If any of the flowers cover the photo, use caution when applying the Mod Podge!

3. The opposite page in an album should not be used so it can be protection for the flowers when the book is closed.

You will need

Flowers and foliage
Photo(s)
Scissors
Acid-free glue
Cocktail toothpick
Acid-free photo album
    paper or page
Paintbrush
Mod Podge
X-acto knife
Saying from a greeting
    card

These photos and arrangements are on a sticky white photo album page. The lighter feeling is at top left, the medium in the middle, and the heavier feeling on the bottom. For the top left **photo**, *I used three blue lobelia pointing to the people in the picture, one white clematis recta, and three red bridal wreath florets pointing to the photo in the middle. The middle* **photo** *has three pink deutzia. The bottom* **photo**, *which is the largest, has lily-of-the-valley on either side to resemble a frame. The bottom of the photo is lined with leaves, pink bridal wreath, and pink choisya ternata. The three photos on the page are tied together by pink flowers appearing in all three positions.*

This is in an abstract form (see page 55), with the heaviness toward the bottom of the page, and the lightness toward the top. The **little girl** *on the upper left is "holding" a daisy. Fruit blossoms are used with the* **photo** *on the lower left, as well as scattered around the page. A red cluster of bridal wreath at top right points to a saying from a greeting card; leaves bring attention to the saying. I placed Queen Anne's lace florets in the center, and I used ferns for the* **boys'** *photo on the lower right side.*

Project
Decorating a Mat

*This charming **mat** has an informal look that doesn't take away from the importance of the photo. The pink and orange bridal wreath match the little girl's dress, and the flowers look like they are coming out of her basket. The white choisya ternata and orange deutzia give the arrangement depth.*

*Yellow coreopsis verticillata grandiflora gives this **mat** a formal look. I also used orange bridal wreath florets and white statice. I designed the so it wouldn't take away from the wedding invitation; instead it brings attention to it.*

Note: Design the mat so that it will enhance the subject you are framing. You can cover the entire mat with flowers or just design in certain areas.

You will need

Flowers and foliage
Photo or invitation
Masking tape
White glue (in dish)
Cocktail toothpick
Materials for framing and
    backing (see page 91)

Decorating a mat with pressed flowers enhances a photo or invitation you wish to keep or give as a gift. You can use either complementary or the same colors of flowers to enhance the printing of an invitation or photo. Make sure the mat is acid-free. Use your imagination and have fun!

1. Place the photo or invitation in the mat. Make sure it is balanced on all four sides. Use strips of masking tape to hold the photo or invitation in place.

2. Apply glue to the backs of the flowers and foliage with the toothpick. Press onto the mat.

3. Frame the photo or invitation and mat (see page 98).

STATIONERY

Designing with pressed flowers on different types of paper make attractive stationery. Invitation stock is a good stand-by, but there are several types of paper that can be used, including invitation stock, wrapping paper, wallpaper, and stationery with a mat attached.

Invitation Stock

Use cards and envelopes printers use for invitations. They are usually white or ivory; both work well with flowers. They come in different sizes, but 6-1/2 x 10 inches (6-1/2 x 5 inches when folded) is the most common. They can be purchased at any printing shop.

*From the left: On the first **card**, three daisies make the vertical line. The purple lythrum gives motion to the arrangement. I also used one pink fruit blossom. The next **card** was designed in a sweeping motion, with the feeling of wind blowing the flowers. Fern was applied as the background, then burgundy cosmos and the orange fruit blossom were added. The lily-of-the-valley spray brings light into the arrangement, and the florets of purple lythrum are good accents. For the **card** on the right, I used heart vine as a base; it gives the arrangement movement. I then added three purple fruit blossoms and a spike of white deutzia. For added color, I used two red choisya ternata, and the fern on the bottom gives the arrangement a solid foundation.*

Wrapping Paper

Wrapping paper can be used for stationery. Because it is not heavy-weight, you must fold it in half, and then in half again, matching corners; this is known as a French fold. When using wrapping paper, choose a muted design; that will not compete with your pressed flower design.

*From the left: The **card** on the left has a spray of fern, with small, medium, and large red fruit blossoms in an the oriental line (see page 53). The three clusters of off-white choisya ternata soften the red. For the next **card**, I used Queen Anne's lace, which picks up the light blue in the paper. I then added a spray of three pink coral bells, as well as three sprays of purple wildflowers to balance the base. The third **card** has a honeysuckle spray as the base for the crescent line arrangement (see page 53). The large burgundy cosmos is the focal point, the white daisy adds to the base line, and purple choisya ternata carries out the line. The cluster of red choisya ternata brings up the height. The final **card** (front right) features a spray of fern, a large white rhododendron as the focal point, a smaller burgundy rhododendron to bring out the pink background of the paper, and purple bridal wreath for contrast.*

Wallpaper

If the wallpaper you choose is heavy enough in weight, it is not necessary to French fold it (see the previous page). Cut the wallpaper a little smaller than the standard size envelope; it should not be so tight that the flowers on the stationery will have to be squeezed into the envelope, which would damage the arrangement. Using a paper cutter will ensure a clean cut.

*For the **card** on the left, I used one large paper white as the focal point. A spray of orange wildflowers and leaves were then added, as was a spray of blue deutzia for contrast. The **card** on the right has one large orange glorisa lily as the focal point, allowing the flower of the wallpaper pattern to point to the arrangement. The curved light purple lythrum brings the eye upward. Finally, the pink cluster of bridal wreath and blue deutzia were added for contrast.*

Stationery With a Mat

Another type of paper that lends itself to a pressed flower arrangement is stationery that has an attached mat. You can use any of the design techniques in Chapter 5, but if the mat has an oval center, a Victorian, s-curve, or crescent-style (see page 53) will work nicely. Because the stationery itself is a standard 5 x 7-inch size, it can also be used as a mat for a picture frame.

*From the left: The first **card** has a spray of orange deutzia as the focal point. Leaves and a spray of purple wildflower and a cluster of white choisya ternata were then added. Finally, a cluster of blue bridal wreath was added for contrast. For the next **card**, I used a fern as the vertical line. I then placed a purple fruit blossom as the focal point, a cluster of white choisya ternata, and a small pink fruit blossom for contrast. The final **card** uses a large burgundy cosmos; its stem complements the oval mat opening. The cluster of orange bridal wreath was then added, as well as a spring of blue wildflower for contrast.*

Design Ideas

Spray painting

Sometimes flowers and foliage will brown out. Instead of throwing them away, place them on newspaper and spray paint them with gold or silver. If they are left on the newspaper too long after they dry, they will begin to curl. To prevent this from happening, make sure the flowers are completely dry, then cover them with newspaper until you are ready to use them so they remain flat. Use them for special birthday, anniversary, or holiday cards. You can design with only gold or silver, or mix gold and silver together.

*Clockwise, from the top: The first **card** has an s-line (see page 53), made up of light and heavy ferns for contrast. The focal point is one large rhododendron. The next **card** has gold leaves and one morning glory as the focal point. The sprig of baby's breath gives height to the arrangement, and the three curved Queen Anne's lace florets create a flow. The next **card** uses a right-angle line (see page 54) with the leaves. It is followed through with the deutzia on top, then the fruit blossom and bridal wreath. I also used a cluster of bridal wreath placed diagonally. For the final **card**, I mixed silver fern with three gold fruit blossoms.*

Glitter Paint

Another type of design with pressed flowers is using glitter craft paint, which comes in a variety of colors and is available at craft stores. Free-hand any symbol imaginable on your stationery. After the paint has dried, you can add pressed flowers.

Tip:

Such common craft items as lace, ribbon, and sequins can be used to enhance your stationery.

---

*From top right: The **blue background card** features gold glitter for a Star of David. It also has fern and three pink deutzia. The **lavender background card** at left has a red glitter heart with one deep purple and lavender Johnny-jump-up and clusters of pink and white choisya ternata. The **card with the green background** on the bottom has a green glitter cross, along with a spray of fern and a red choisya ternata.*

*This **invitation** uses an orange cosmos for the focal point. A lily-of-the-valley is on one side, and lythrum is on the other.*

INVITATIONS

Pressed flowers on any type of invitation are beautiful. Your guests will be delighted to receive these special invitations that can be framed as keepsakes.

If you order pre-printed invitations from a printing shop, the engraving is printed on a flat cardboard-like surface to the right side of the card. Make sure there are 2 to 3 inches for the pressed flower design. Any line arrangement will be attractive. You can choose the color for the printing or background paper. If the printing or border is a color, try to include some of the same color flowers as the printing or the border (except black). This will tie it all together. If the printing is black, any color combination will be beautiful.

You can also purchase stock yourself at a printing shop. If you do this, and you have a computer, try designing your own invitation.

When gluing flowers to stationery, it is important to have a heavy piece of wood to keep the flowers in place while the glue is drying. If too much glue is put on the flowers without first blotting, the paper will stick to the wooden weight; when it is removed, it will tear the paper.

If you want to frame a special invitation, follow the instructions on page 98.

*This **invitation** has a heart vine base. One large pink fruit blossom is centered, three purple wildflowers were added for contrast, and one yellow coreopsis verticillata grandiflora brings up the height and adds a light feeling to the invitation.*

*This **invitation** features one large burgundy cosmos with one orange fruit blossom on the right and orange blossom buds on the left. One blue lobelia gives contrast. The thin leaf points upward toward the flower and invitation.*

Project

TECHNIQUE FOR GLUING FLOWERS ON STATIONERY AND INVITATIONS

1. Apply glue to the backs of the flowers and foliage with the toothpick. Press onto the paper. If the stems lift, add more glue with the toothpick.

2. After gluing flowers on paper, it is important to have a heavy piece of wood (like a 2 x 4) to keep the flowers flat. Place the wood on the paper for no longer than five minutes. If it is not removed, dried glue on the paper will cause it to stick to the wood and therefore tear it. Should any glue run on the paper, blot it immediately with a white tissue before the wooden weight is placed. If this is not done, the next time you use the wooden weight it will attach itself to areas and can ruin other work. When finished with a design and the wood is removed, do not stack one on top of another until you are sure they are completely dry.

3. If the flowers are dyed, be very careful when you place them. Once they are on the paper, they cannot be removed (the color will remain).

4. If sending your creation, write "Hand Stamp" on the envelope.

*I complemented the deep red printing on this **invitation** with deep red fruit blossoms, and softened the color by adding a large white daisy and small light lavender fruit blossoms. I balanced the overall picture by designing the larger arrangement to the left and the smaller arrangement to the right of the printing. The off-white mat softens the deep red color, bringing harmony and balance to the invitation. (To frame an invitation, see page 98.)*

*For this **invitation**, I used two asparagus ferns, one pointing up and the other toward the invitation. The lily-of-the-valley also points toward it. Three dark blue Johnny-jump-ups and a pink fruit blossom were added for contrast.*

Project

INITIAL STATIONERY

For the "B" card on the left, I simply used sprayed gold fern. The other "B" card has small leaves curving around the paper. Pink deutzia buds were then added, along with yellow florets of Queen Anne's lace. For the "P" card, I drew the "P" first. Instead of filling it in with flowers, I arranged orange fruit blossoms, a cluster of white choisya ternata, and a sprig of purple wildflower around it.

There is a certain freedom that comes when designing with pressed flowers on stationery—there are no basic rules to follow. Flowers can be placed on the right or left side of the paper, in the center, or on the top or bottom. Here we are going to design initial stationery. The following are three different options: with the first you place flowers inside of the outline, with the second you follow the shape of the initial, and with the third you can do a more abstract design.

You will need

Flowers and foliage
Pencil
Optional: Black ink (water-proof)
White glue (in dish)
Cocktail toothpick
Piece of stationery

Method 1

1. With a pencil, draw the initial on the stationery. Optional: Outline the initial in black ink.

2. Apply glue to the backs of individual petals or small flowers and foliage with the toothpick. Press them inside of the initial.

Method 2

1. With a pencil, draw the initial on the stationery. Outline the initial with black ink.

2. Apply glue to the backs of the flowers and foliage with the toothpick. Press them onto the paper, following the shape of the initial or on the outside of it.

Method 3

1. With a pencil, draw the initial on the stationery. Outline the initial with black ink.

2. Apply glue to the backs of the flowers and foliage with the toothpick. Place the flowers and foliage in an abstract design around the initial (don't fill the entire initial in).

Oriental Collage

Collage is an artistic composition of materials and objects combined on a surface, often with unifying lines and color. Leaves, ferns, and grasses are important features in oriental design, as mentioned in Chapter 5. Oriental collage is a method of applying these elements as a collage, covered with oriental paper. It is a method that can be used for designing pictures, bookmarks, lampshades, window decorations, gift boxes, and perfume bottles. It is a charming project where simplicity is key; the end result should be as if nature was brought into your home.

PROJECT LIST

ORIENTAL COLLAGE PICTURE

*This **picture** has several layers of rice papers. After placing them, I added color. Asparagus fern was applied first to give the feeling of lightness reaching upward. Then, heavier leaves were filled in, and finally yellow coreopsis verticillata grandiflora leaves were added. There is a contrast between the lighter and darker leaves. The two birds were cut from a magazine and placed on the fern to bring attention to the center of the picture.*

For this project, you will be doing a watercolor wash (see page 93). When I do it, I apply, for example, purple to the background, clean my brush, and then apply a little blue. They will run together slightly run, blending the two colors. I also add a touch of green here and there, blending into another color. Any color combination can be used. An abstract application is better rather than covering the entire surface of your project.

You will be applying various layers of papers onto the surface of your project. The papers you will use include Sumi-e paper, which is a white rice paper, Natsume paper, a white-on-white fibrous paper, and Sakuragami, which is a very thin paper (a white paper napkin can be used in place of this).

A color wheel, which indicates the results when two primary colors are mixed together, is a handy tool (see page 58). The primary colors are red, yellow, and blue. When mixing two of the primary colors together, the end result is a secondary color:

Red + yellow = orange

Yellow + blue = green

Blue + red = violet

Different hues can result from different amounts of each color used.

1. Place a few layers of newspaper on your work area.

2. Do a watercolor wash (see page 93). Don't cover the entire surface; it should look natural, not painted. Blending colors is very effective. Let dry completely.

3. Tear the Sumi-e paper to the desired size of the your finished picture.

4. Make a mixture of one-third white glue and two-thirds water in the dish. With the soft flat brush, cover the entire surface of the paper with the mixture.

5. Place the ferns, leaves, and grasses on the wet surface of the paper in the desired design. Optional: Scatter seeds on the surface of the paper.

6. Before the glue has a chance to dry, tear pieces of Natsume paper in uneven shapes and place them in different areas, using the glue-water mixture to cover that surface. Overlapping the papers will add dimension to the piece.

7. With the bristle brush or toothbrush, gently press in a stamping position toward the edge of the paper. Make sure that the corners are secured (if they are not, they will eventually curl and break). If areas of the paper tear during this process, add more of the Natsume paper; simply dip the soft brush into the glue-water mixture and add to the areas that need to be filled.

8. Before the glue has a chance to dry, cover with torn pieces in uneven shapes of Sakuragami veil paper or white paper napkin; place them in different positions over your design. If it becomes a little wrinkled in spots, it will add charm to your design. Hold the firm brush or toothbrush upright in a stamping position and gently press the bristles downward to adhere the veil paper to the entire background. Again, overlapping papers will enhance the appearance. When securing the Sakuragami paper, be very careful around the leaves or ferns; too much pressure will tear the paper. Make sure the outlines of the ferns show. At this point, you will not be able to see the Sakuragami paper that was covering the ferns or leaves.

9. Leave the finished piece to almost dry. At this time, you can gently press any air pockets in place with your finger or the toothbrush.

10. When the piece is completely dry, sandwich it between two pieces of waxed paper and place it into a telephone book. If your picture is too large for a telephone book, cut two pieces of large cardboard and waxed paper to the size you require. Sandwich the piece between them and put a heavy weight on top; this will ensure that your project remains flat.

11. Frame the picture (see page 98).

You will need

Ferns, leaves, and grasses
Newspapers
Watercolor paper
Materials for a watercolor wash (see page 93)
Sumi-e paper
White glue (in dish)
Water
Optional: Seeds
Flat brush with soft bristles
Natsume paper
Flat brush with firm bristles (A toothbrush with firm bristles can be used)
Sakuragami or a white paper napkin
Waxed paper and telephone book or two pieces of cardboard and a heavy weight
Materials for framing and backing (see page 91)

Project

LAMPSHADE

You can use the oriental collage technique to design a one-of-a-kind lampshade. Any color combination that suits your decor will be outstanding. A slightly curved lampshade can be used. A burlap shade will require several layers of Sumi-e paper and will absorb much of the glue-water mixture (hence the shade will become very wet), but if you are patient, you can use one.

1. Cover your work area with several sheets of newspaper.

2. Dip the soft brush into a glue-water mixture (see the previous page, Step 4) and brush it onto the portion of the shade you will be covering with ferns and foliage.

3. Tear uneven pieces of Sumi-e paper and place them on the lampshade. Continue until the entire glued portion of the lampshade is covered. Brush glue over the torn pieces. If they start to pucker, resulting in small streaks, it is okay because it will give the lampshade a background texture.

4. Optional: You can do a watercolor wash after the lampshade is dry.

5. With the soft flat brush, cover the backs of the leaves and ferns with the glue-water mixture and place them in the desired areas. Continue until you are satisfied with the design. Optional: Attach seeds to the surface of the lampshade.

6. Tear pieces of Sakuragami paper or white napkin to cover the leaves and fern. Dip the flat brush into the glue-water solution and brush onto the paper or napkin. With the brush with firm bristles or toothbrush, gently, with a stamping motion, touch the leaves you just placed on the paper. If there is too much water in the paper, it will tear. If this should occur, simply tear another piece of paper or napkin and affix with the flat brush. Make sure the outlines of the leaves are visible.

7. Let the lampshade dry overnight.

*First, rice papers were applied, then a blended watercolor wash was applied to the **lampshade** that coordinated with the lamp base's colors. One large fern is in the center. Two different types are on either end, pointing inward. Heavier-textured leaves are on either side, and more leaves are at the base. Seeds are present at the base; they contribute a heavier feeling to the base.*

You will need

Ferns, leaves, and grasses
Newspapers
Flat brush with soft bristles
White glue (in dish)
Water
Lampshade
Optional: Watercolor wash materials (see page 93)
Sumi-e paper
Optional: Seeds
Sakuragami or a white paper napkin
Flat brush with firm bristles (A toothbrush with firm bristles can be used)

OTHER APPLICATIONS

You can also use the oriental collage technique on such items as bottles and gift boxes. Have fun experimenting on different surfaces with this simple yet beautiful technique.

Simple oriental collage **stationery** *can make a bold statement if you just use a few pieces of fern. First, I applied rice paper, then did a watercolor wash. Finally, I added four fern pieces.*

From the left: For the **large bottle** *at left, I applied rice paper and then used lavender, orange, and a little blue watercolor. I added curved asparagus fern and placed a heavy leaf and a medium leaf under that. Finally, I covered it with rice paper and sprayed it with Krylon. For the* **small square bottle**, *I first applied rice paper and then I brushed on pink and purple watercolor. Next, I added some fern, covered it with rice paper, and put on a heart sticker. To give the bottle luster, I sprayed it with Krylon. After applying the layer of rice paper on the* **rectangular bottle**, *I added yellow and green watercolor for the background, then the asparagus fern. I added a small cluster of white choisya ternata and a small leaf, covered it with rice paper, and sprayed it with Krylon.*

The **bookmark** *made from blue construction paper on the left has three leaves, with the smaller one balancing the two larger ones. The gold cord adds interest to the bookmark. The* **bookmark** *on the right has a white background with one asparagus fern; the green ribbon brings it together.*

CONCLUSION

I AM the Flower

I AM the flower in the desert
I AM the flower in the sand
I AM the flower
Touched
By God's hand.

Bernice Wechsler Peitzer

It is a joy to share with you what was given to me. You will bloom together with the flowers. Your life will change and you will become more fulfilled in every way.

Through the joy of discovering new things, your world will unfold. The feeling that will come to you when you hold a flower in your hand and really look at it for the very first time is a revelation. The beauty spreads from the flower to you, and you cannot help but feel a part of this magnificent creation. It is yours to have and to share.

Have good days.

Floral Symbolism

If you are making a gift for a special occasion, why not make it out of flowers that express your feelings, commemorate the event, or describe the lucky recipient? The following list was derived from numerous sources, including the wonderful book *The Language of Flowers* by Margaret Pickston.

Aster: Virgil
Azaleas: Temperance, moderation
Bachelor's buttons: Blessedness, sacredness
Begonia: Negative thoughts
Bittersweet: Truth, honesty
Bridal wreath: Happiness and love
Buttercup: Childishness, immaturity
Campanula: Gratitude, thankfulness
Candytuft: Indifference
Carnation: Warm-hearted affection; preserves the body and keeps the mind from fearful dreams
Chrysanthemum: Gold = good for depression; red = love; yellow = slighted love; white = truth
Cloves: Dignity
Clover (four-leaf): Be mine, possessiveness
Columbine: Folly; purple = resolution, determination; red = anxiety
Cornflower: Faithfulness
Crocus: Cheerfulness
Dahlia: Instability
Daffodil: Regard; yellow = chivalry
Daisy: Measure of love, perception, innocence
Dogwood: Durability, lasting
Fern: Security, sincerity
Forget-me-not: True love
French marigold: Jealousy
Goldenrod: Encouragement
Grape (wild): Charity
Hibiscus: Delicate beauty
Honesty: Honesty
Honeysuckle: Lasting love, good disposition
Hyacinth: Play; purple = sadness; blue = constancy; white = continued gentleness
Ivy: Friendship
Larkspur: Lightness; pink = fickleness; purple = lofty and arrogant
Laurel: Glory, splendor
Lavender: Keeps away evil spirits and flies
Leaves (falling): As many as you can catch will ensure an equal number of happy months; oak = bravery
Leaves (dead): Melancholy
Lemon: Zest
Lemon blossoms: Fidelity in love
Lilac: Purple = new emotions of love, white = young innocence
Lily (day): Innocence, joyousness; yellow = falsehood, gaiety
Lily-of-the-valley: Return to happiness

Lobelia: Malicious
Lotus: Eloquence
Lotus flower: Estranged love
Marigold: Grief, despair
Mint: Virtue
Mock orange: Counterfeit, untrue
Morning glory: Affection
Moss: Maternal love
Mustard seed: Indifference
Myrtle: Love
Narcissus: Egotism
Nasturtium: Patriotism
Orange flowers: Chastity, pure
Palm: Victory, success
Pansy: Thoughts
Parsley: Festivity
Patience: Patience
Passion flower: Religious superstition
Peony: Shame, bashfulness
Peppermint: Warmth of feeling
Petunia: Never despair
Periwinkle: Blue = young friendship; white = pleasing memories
Phlox: Unanimity, agreement of mind
Poppy (oriental): Silence; red = consolation; white = sleep
Primrose: Evening, inconstancy, incompatible
Purple flowers: Color of mourning
Quince: Temptation
Red and white flowers: Omen of death
Rhubarb: Give advice
Rose: Love, ambition celebrated in poetry
Salvia: Blue = thinking of you; red = forever
Shamrock: Light-heartedness
Star of Bethlehem: Purity
Stock: Lasting beauty
Strawberry blossom: Foresight
Sweet basil: Good wishes
Sweet pea: Delicate pleasure
Sweet William: Gallantry
Thyme: Activity
Tulip: Red = declaration of love; variegated = beautiful eyes; yellow = hopeless love
Verbena: Scarlet = sensibility; white = pure
Violet: Faithfulness
Virginia Creeper: Ever changing
Water lily: Purity of heart
Weigela: Faithful
Wisteria: Clinging
Yellow flowers: Reflect the sun
Zinnia: Thinking of distant friends

Sources:
"Mayflowers Flower Symbolism." 1997. www.mayflowers.net
Pickston, Margaret. *The Language of Flowers*. London: Michael Joseph, Ltd. 1968.
"Say It With Flowers." www.brownsflorist.com

Appendix 2
Herbal Health

The nature of plants are directly related to the gods or the moon, sun, or stars. Their uses have long involved the study of astrology and medicine. Magicians of days gone by used them to cast spells, both good and evil, and Native Americans used them for medicine and healing. In recent years, there has been renewed interested in using seeds, leaves, roots, and barks as medicine. This section is intended to be a guide; please consult a physician before taking any of the items listed in this section.

Be aware that the quality of herbs vary. When choosing the herb, be sure it is the best quality and its date has not expired. Make sure the brand has been scientifically tested. Read the instructions on the bottle carefully to see what you are getting in each dose and purchase your herbs at a reliable pharmacy or health store.

Benefits of Herbs

Herbs can have many positive effects on one's body. They can cleanse and purify the body without side effects, normalize body functions, they are extremely nutritional (high in vitamins, minerals, and other nutrients), raise the body's energy level, and stimulate the body's immune system.

Vitamins and Minerals

Many plants contain vitamins, minerals, and trace minerals. Herbs are a great source of vitamins and minerals because the body can usually digest them easier than those of fish or animal origin.

Vitamins

Vitamin A: Alfalfa, Black Cohosh, Cayenne, Eyebright, Red Clover, Saw Palmetto Berries, Yarrow, Yellow Dock

Vitamin B: Blue Cohosh, Cascara Sagrada, Fenugreek, Hawthorne, Licorice, Papaya

Vitamin C: Bee Pollen, Chickweed, Comfrey, Echinacea, Garlic, Golden Seal, Juniper Berries, Peppermint, Rose Hips

Vitamin D: Alfalfa, Dandelion, Red Raspberry, Rose Hips, Sarsaparilla

Vitamin E: Burdock, Comfrey, Dong Quai, Kelp, Skullcap, Slippery Elm, Yarrow

Vitamin F: Red Raspberry, Slippery Elm

Vitamin K: Alfalfa, Gota Kola, Yarrow

Minerals

Calcium: Aloe, Cayenne, Chamomile, Fennel, Marshmallow, Sage, White Oak Bark.

Cobalt: Dandelion, Horsetail, Juniper Berries, Lobelia, Parsley, Red Clover, White Oak Bark

Iodine: Bladderwack (Seawrack), Kelp

Caution:

Some herbs contain active ingredients that make them unfit for consumption in large quantities, including
Oxalates: sorrel
Safrole: sassafras and massoia
Thujone: tansy and wormwood
Tannins: myrtle

The following herbs and remedies are listed for informational purposes only. ***Consult a physician before consuming any herbs.***

Iron: Burdock, Chickweed, Ginseng, Hops, Mullein, Nesttles, Parsley, Peppermint, Rosemary, Sarsaparilla, Scullcap, Yellow Dock

Magnesium: Alfalfa, Catnip, Ginger, Gota Kola, Red Clover, Rosemary, Valerian, Wood Betony

Potassium: Aloe, Blue Cohosh, Cayenne, Cascara Sagrada, Chaparral, Fennel, Golden Seal, Parsley, Rose Hips, Slippery Elm, Valerian, Yarrow

Zinc: Burdock, Chamomile, Dandelion, Eyebright, Hawthorne, Licorice, Marshmallow, Sarsaparilla

Trace Minerals

Alfalfa, Black Cohosh, Burdock, Cascara Sagrada, Chaparral, Dandelion, Hawthorne, Horsetail, Kelp, Lobelia, Parsley, Red Clover, Rose Hips, Sage, Sarsaparilla, Valerian, Yellow Dock

General Benefits

The following is a listing of herbs, their uses, and benefits.

Alfalfa: Alfalfa is a good source of carotene (vitamin A). It is useful in reducing fevers and is very beneficial to the blood, acting as a blood purifier. Contains natural fluoride, preventing tooth decay and helps rebuild decayed teeth.

Aloe: A great healing agency. Works wonderfully in cleaning out the colon; gives regular bowel movements. Aloe works well on any kind of sore on the outside of the body. Excellent remedy for piles and hemorrhoids.

Angelica root: Remedy to strengthen the heart. Excellent in diseases of the lungs and heart. With regular use of angelica, there is a distaste for alcoholic drinks. Good for stomach troubles, heartburn, and gas.

Barberry bark: Acts on bile, bad breath, digestion, kidneys, liver, rheumatism, skin, and a gargle for a sore throat.

Bay leaf: Gives tone and strength to the digestive organs and is good for cramps.

Bilberry leaf: Bilberry strengthens fine capillaries that feed eye muscles and nerves, reducing and even reversing the damage caused by blood vessel deterioration. Increases night vision and reduces eye fatigue.

Blackberry leaf: A good tea. Great for diarrhea and healing wounds.

Black cohosh: Excellent for regulating menstrual flow and cramps. Contains natural estrogen. Has no cancer causing agents like synthetic estrogen.

Blessed thistle (holy thistle): A stimulant tonic for the stomach and heart. Aids circulation and helps resolve liver problems. Takes oxygen to the brain and strengthens memory.

Blue flag: Has been useful in the treatment of cancer, rheumatism, constipation, skin diseases, impurity of blood, and liver troubles.

Blue violet: Relieves severe headaches and congestion in the head. Cleans out mucus in the system. Effective in healing and giving prompt relief of internal ulcers.

Boldo leaf: Stimulated digestion and secretion of bile. Useful for treating gallstones. Recommended for liver problems.

Boneset: Good for colds and flu. Taken for a cold, the infusion has a tonic and mild laxative effect.

Borage leaf: Reduces high fevers. Good for irritation of skin and lung problems.

Capsicum (cayenne): Normalizes blood pressure and the circulatory system. Feeds the cell structure of arteries, veins, and capillaries so they can regain elasticity. A good stimulant, allowing the healing and cleansing processes to start. Stops bleeding on contact.

Caraway seed: Strengthens and gives tone to and prevents fermentation in the stomach. Aids in digestion.

Celery leaf and seed: Effective for incontinence of urine. Good for rheumatism and nervousness.

Chamomile flower: Excellent for a nervous stomach. Can be used to relieve cramping associated with the menstrual cycle.

Chervil: A mild diuretic. Lowers blood pressure.

Chickweed: Rich in vitamin C and minerals, especially calcium, magnesium, and potassium. Helps discharge toxins. A good blood purifier. Heals and soothes everything. Dissolves plaque in blood vessels.

Cinnamon bark: Takes the sting away from cuts and scrapes. Aids in breaking down fats during digestion.

Coltsfoot herb and flower: Soothing to the mucous membrane. Improves troubles with lungs, relieves phlegm, and is useful for coughs.

Dandelion leaf and root: Helps detoxify any poisons in the liver. Has been beneficial in lowering blood pressure.

Echinacea root: Aids in glandular infections. Used to treat strep throat, lymph glands, and cleans morbid matter from the stomach. Helps with colds and flu. Expels poisons and toxins.

Elecampane root: Used in the first stages of a cold or flu.

Fenugreek seed: Used for allergies, coughs, digestion, emphysema, headaches, intestinal inflammation, and sore throats.

Feverfew: Helps with migraine.

Garlic: Good for cholesterol and infections.

Ginger root: Helpful for stimulating the circulatory system and for sore throat. Has a cleansing effect on the kidneys and bowels.

Ginko: Used for cognitive deficiency.

Ginseng root, Siberian: Used to build resistance against stress, both mental and physical. Some people call it the slow aging process. Reduces vitality.

Golden seal, tops, root, and leaf: Used for bladder infections, bronchitis, cankers, coughs, colds, earaches, inflammation, mouth sores, mucous membrane, nasal passages, and ulcers.

Gota kola: Known as the memory herb. Stimulates circulation to the brain and is a nerve tonic.

Grapeseed, green tea, or pine bark extract: Oxidative tissue damage.

Hawthorne leaf: Good for people under stress and effective in relieving insomnia.

Hops flower: Produces sleep and decreases the desire for alcohol.

Horsetail (shavegrass): Makes fingernails and hair strong. Fractured bones should heal faster. Good for eyes, ear, nose, throat, and glandular disorders.

Hydrangea root: For backaches caused by kidney trouble and good for bladder problems.

Kava kava root: Induces sleep and helps nervousness. When taken at night will induce restful sleep. Good for anxiety.

Kelp: Has a high content of iodine. Helps fight infection. Excellent for nails and hair.

Lady's slipper root: For recurring headaches. Also for liver or stomach problems. Combine it with chamomile.

Lavender flower: Relaxes the body.

Licorice root: Works as a mild laxative. Will strengthen circulatory system. Helps to put vitality into the body. Used for throat and injured muscles.

Malva flower: Helps soothe inflammation in the mouth and throat. Helpful for earaches.

Marjoram: Good for general aches and pains. Combine with chamomile and gentian. Beneficial for sour stomach or loss of appetite.

Milk thistle herb: Good as a detoxifier and liver disorders.

Mullen leaf: Helps pulmonary ailments and strengthen sinuses. Effective in relieving swollen joints.

Nettle leaf: Together with seawrack, will bring good results in weight loss. Tea is good for fevers and colds. Good for dandruff and will bring back the natural color of hair.

Nutmeg: Used to prevent gas.

Papaya leaf: Useful as a digestive stimulant. Relieves sour stomach.

Parsley leaf: For ailments of the liver. Good for blood vessels, capillaries, and arterioles.

Peppermint leaf: Good for headaches. Entire system will work more normally.

Periwinkle: Tea can be used for nervous condition. Good remedy for diarrhea.

Plantain leaf: Good for all infections and chronic skin problems. Also for hemorrhoids and inflammations.

Red clover tops: Entire body system will benefit. Excellent to purify the blood. Good results against acne and other skin problems.

Rose hips: Infection fighter. Good for stress.

Rosemary: Excellent for colds, coughs, and nervous headaches. Good results for sores around the mouth.

Safflower: Prevents and helps eliminate the buildup of uric and lactic acid in the body.

Saffron: Soothes the digestive tract. Can relieve gout and arthritis. Promotes perspiration; helpful in colds.

Sage leaf: Gives circulation to the heart. Good remedy for stomach troubles. Used for complaints in poor digestion. Useful as a hair tonic.

Sarsaparilla root: Has a useful effect on the blood system. Excellent for all skin disorders. Stimulates the action of the liver to clear toxins from the body.

Saw palmetto: Prostate disease.

Seawrack (bladderwack): Good herb to combat obesity. Has good effect on glandular afflictions.

Shepherd's purse: Remedy for diarrhea.

Solomon's seal root: Used for external problems. Makes a good poultice for bruises. Can be used as a wash for skin problems and blemishes.

Spearmint leaf: Relieves suppressed, painful, or scalding urine. Helpful for gas in stomach. Very quieting and soothing for the nerves.

Squaw vine: Useful for the treatment of water retention. When used as a wash, gives relief to sore eyes.

Star anise: Promotes appetite and relieves flatulence.

St. John's wort: Powerful as a blood purifier. Good in cases of tumors and boils. Good in chronic uterine problems. Will correct irregular menstruation. Used for depression.

Summer savory leaf: Useful in treating diarrhea, upset stomach, and sore throat.

Thyme leaf: Removes mucus from the head, lung, and respiratory passages. Fights infection. Relief to migraine headaches.

Valerian root: Healing effect on the nervous system. Very quieting and calming. Good for entire circulatory system. Promotes sleep if taken as a tea at night. (Note: Never boil valerian root.)

White willow bark: Useful for all stomach troubles, especially sour stomach and heartburn. Used for minor aches and pains in the body.

Wild alum root (cranesbill): Powerful astringent for the body. Useful in cholera, diarrhea, and dysentery. Used as a rinse for sores in the mouth and bleeding gums. Powder sprinkled on a wound or cut will help stop bleeding. Excellent to rid mucus and pus in the bladder and intestines.

Wild yam root: Very relaxing and soothing to the nerves for people who get excited easily. Helps expel gas from the stomach and bowels.

Witch hazel bark and leaf: Restores circulation. Use for stiff joints.

Yarrow root: Heavily used at the onset, a cold usually breaks up within 24 hours. Has a healing and soothing effect on the mucous membranes.

Yellow doc root: Blood purifier. Good for all skin problems. Helps tone entire system. Excellent cleansing herb for the lymphatic system. Endurance builder.

Yerba santa: Excellent for bronchial congestion, as well as chest conditions. Effective when there is much discharge from the nose. Good for rheumatism.

Yucca root: Reduces inflammation of the joints. Helpful for arthritic and rheumatoid problems. Excellent shampoo.

Sources:
Forsell, Mary and Rosemary Verey. *Heirloom Herbs: Using Old-fashioned Herbs in Gardens, Recipes, and Decorations*. New York: Villard Books. 1991.
Hylton, William. *The Rodale Herb Book*. Emmaus, PA: Rodale Press, Inc.
McVicar, Jekka. *Herbs for the Home*. New York: Viking Penguin. 1995.
Turcotte, Patricia. *The New England Herb Gardener*. Woodstock, VT: Countryman Press. 1991.
"A Useful Guide to Herbal Health Care." Health Center for Better Living, Inc. Naples, Florida.

GLOSSARY

Abstract design: A design that has no formal line.

Accent: A sharp contrast between color, size, and form.

Balance: Stability in a design.

Bale: A jewelry finding that is attached to an object for a chain to go through.

Brad: A short nail.

Conditioning: The time it takes for a flower to be pressed.

Collage: An artistic composition of materials and objects pasted over a surface with unifying lines and color.

Complementary colors: Colors that are opposite each other on the color wheel.

Depth: The act of feeling the inward distance as you look into a picture.

Focal point: The center of interest in an arrangement.

Finding: A jeweler's term for individual pieces or materials.

Germination: The process of seeds sprouting roots and leaves.

Heirloom variety: Old, scarce varieties that are not easily found in garden shops.

Harmony: Plant material working together to make a unified whole.

Jump ring: A circular finding that prevents a pendant from turning.

Line arrangement: A particular type of flower arrangement, for example vertical or horizontal.

Oriental arrangement: Consists of three levels: top level represents heaven, middle level represents man, and the lower level represents earth.

Potpourri: A mixture of scented flowers and petals.

Rhythm: A feeling of natural flow.

Scale: The size relationship of the flowers in an arrangement.

Succulent plants: Plants that contain an unusual amount of water.

Victorian arrangement: Flower arrangement that is designed in either a round or oval shape.

ESOURCES

Design Master, Color Tool, Inc.
P.O. Box 601
Boulder, CO 80306
303-443-5214
www.dmcolor.com
Just For Flowers

Dorothy Biddle Service
348 Greeley Lake Rd.
Greeley, PA 18425-9799
570-226-3239
www.dorothybiddle.com
Shears

Michael's Invitations, Inc.
4050C Skyron Dr.
P.O. Box 1137
Doylestown, PA 18901
www.michael'sinvitations.com
Invitations and card stock

Shady Lady
P.O. Box 523
Menasha, WI 54952-0523
1-888-722-7798
www.Shades4fun
Lampshades

Sunstone, Inc.
P.O. Box 788
Cooperstown, NY 13326-0788
1-800-327-0306
Flower presses

THE
History of
the Jewish People

A Story of Tradition and Change

Jonathan B. Krasner and Jonathan D. Sarna

EDITORIAL ADVISORS

Gail Beckman Buchbinder

Rabbi Martin S. Cohen

Rabbi Barry Diamond

Professor Amy-Jill Levine

Nina Price, R. J. E.

Behrman House Publishers
www.behrmanhouse.com

Project Manager: Gila Gevirtz
Designer: Stacey May
Cartographer: Jim McMahon
Photographic Research: Lauryn Silverhardt Tuchman
Cartographic Consultant: Dr. Itzik Eshel

The Publisher and authors gratefully acknowledge the generous editorial contributions made by Marc Z. Brettler, Shaye Cohen, Michael Cook, and Ruth Langer to the development of *The History of the Jewish People.*

The Publisher gratefully acknowledges the cooperation of the following sources of photographs and graphic images: American Jewish Archives, Cincinnati Campus, HUC-JIR: 164; American Jewish Historical Society: 104 (bottom), 160; Beth Hatefusoth Museum of the Jewish Diaspora: 18 (bottom); Bildarchiv Preussischer Kulturbesitz/Art Resource, NY: v (bottom), 134; Bridgeman-Giraudon/Art Resources, NY: 75, 76, 79, 94; Corbis: compass on cover, magnifying glass on chapter openers, iii, 72; Creative Image Photography: 14, 24, 126; Frank J. Darmstaedter: 20 (top); Doré: 8, 25; Werner Forman/Art Resources, NY: 62–63, 68; Foto Marburg/Art Resources, NY: 82; Gila Gevirtz: 5, 12, 37, 53 (bottom), 60, 64, 118, 135, 141; The Granger Collection, NY: iv, 2, 16–18, 35, 48 (bottom), 51, 57, 86–89, 96, 99, 101, 108, 123, 125, 136, 147; Israel Ministry of Tourism: 28–29, 38, 55, 116; The Jewish Museum/Art Resources, NY: v (top circle), 22, 103, 110–111, 113 (top); Terry Kaye: 69 (left), 78, 90, 149; Saul H. Landa: 93; Erich Lessing/Art Resources, NY: 6–7, 9, 13, 26, 31, 33, 36, 41, 42 (top left), 48 (top), 53 (top), 54, 113 (bottom), 117, 119, 132–133, 142, 154–155, 162; Richard Lobell: vi, 1, 105, 165; Ratner Center for the Study of Conservative Judaism, JTS: 165; Elizabeth Reade Photography: 47; Réunion des Musées Nationaux/Art Resources, NY: 4; Scala/Art Resources, NY: 42 (top right), 95; Snark/Art Resource, NY: 144–145, 148; Ginny Twersky 20 (bottom), 70, 137; Vanni/Art Resources, NY: 100; Bildarchiv Preussischer Kulturbesitz/Art Resource, Doré, Gila Gevirtz, The Granger Collection, Israel Ministry of Tourism: cover images.

Copyright © 2006 by Behrman House, Inc.
ISBN: 978-0-87441-190-4
Published by Behrman House, Inc.
Springfield, NJ 07081
www.behrmanhouse.com
Manufactured in the United States of America

Library of Congress Cataloging-in-Publication Data
Krasner, Jonathan B.
   The history of the Jewish people : a story of tradition and change/
Jonathan B. Krasner and Jonathan D. Sarna.
      v. cm.
   Includes index.
   Contents: v. 1. Ancient Israel to 1880's America.
   ISBN 0-87441-190-4 (v. 1)
   1. Jews—History—Juvenile literature. I. Sarna, Jonathan D.
II. Title.
DS118. K735 2006
909'.04924—dc22

2005037140